ENTERED JUL 3 0 2004

Cinema and Life Development

Cinema and Life Development

Healing Lives and Training Therapists

Thomas H. Peake

Westport, Connecticut
London

Library of Congress Cataloging-in-Publication Data

Peake, Tom H.
   Cinema and life development : healing lives and training therapists / Thomas H. Peake.
      p. cm.
   Includes bibliographical references and index.
   ISBN 0-275-97500-2 (alk. paper)
   1. Motion pictures in psychotherapy. 2. Motion pictures—Psychological aspects. I. Title.
RC489.M654P43 2004
   616.89'14—dc21   2003048226

British Library Cataloguing in Publication Data is available.

Copyright © 2004 by Thomas H. Peake

All rights reserved. No portion of this book may be
reproduced, by any process or technique, without the
express written consent of the publisher.

Library of Congress Catalog Card Number: 2003048226
ISBN: 0-275-97500-2

First published in 2004

Praeger Publishers, 88 Post Road West, Westport, CT 06881
An imprint of Greenwood Publishing Group, Inc.
www.praeger.com

Printed in the United States of America

The paper used in this book complies with the
Permanent Paper Standard issued by the National
Information Standards Organization (Z39.48-1984).

10 9 8 7 6 5 4 3 2 1

Copyright Acknowledgments

The author and publisher gratefully acknowledge permission to quote from the following:

"In My Craft or Sullen Art," (excerpts) by Dylan Thomas, from *The Poems of Dylan Thomas*, copyright ©1946 by New Directions Publishing Corp. Reprinted by permission of New Directions Publishing Corp. Used by permission of New Directions Publishing Corp.

Frank, Jerome D., M.D., Ph.D., and Julia B. Frank, M.D. *Persuasion and Healing: A Comparative Study of Psychotherapy*, pp. 40–43, ©1991 The Johns Hopkins University Press. Reprinted with permission of The Johns Hopkins University Press.

The quotation from, *Who's Afraid of Virginia Woolf?* by Edward Albee, is reprinted with the permission of Scribner, an imprint of Simon and Schuster Adult Publishing Group. Copyright © 1962 Edward Albee.

Contents

Acknowledgments		vii
Introduction: Challenges, Themes, and Solutions		1
1.	Life Span Development: Cornerstones and Scaffolding	11
2.	The Power and Possibilities of Cinema	33
3.	Medical, Spiritual, and Psychological Dimensions	43
4.	Dueling Motives: Culture, Gender, and Generation T. Peake and B. Nussbaum	57
5.	Humor, Hungers, and Health	75
6.	Generational Resonance: To Era Is Human, to Forgive, Divine	85
7.	Training Therapists: Hearing, Discerning, and Revising Life Stories—Using Images Generated from Valuable and Favorite Movies	93
8.	Diversions, Fascinations, and Awards	113
Select Bibliography		123
Subject Index		129
Movie Index		137

Acknowledgments

This book is the culmination of a number of years searching for an excuse to watch movies when I should have been doing something "worthwhile." Perhaps the result makes the pleasure legitimate. Good cinema often does not adhere to a clear linear outline (as English teachers urged us to master). Cinema, both good and bad, can have emotionally charged effects and often wise messages. Movies cross the stream between focused logic and the ebbs and tides of dreams. My family has even accused him of having "waterfront property on the *stream of consciousness.*"

With that caveat, it is hoped this book helps people enjoy film and expands the benefits of this rich venue. Perhaps it can enliven some dull classes while discovering landmarks on the multisensory stream of that journey. The value of cinema to show life stages, hopes and fears, dilemmas and solutions, is a rich resource well worth seining.

I am grateful for my wife Vicky's patience and encouragement, plus support from daughters Lisa and Katie. Lori Sorum, Kelly Blair, Karl Sachs, Rita Kronis, Nita Romer, Brian Nussbaum, Andy Dobo, Jim Oelschlager, Mike Kohn, Shari Harwell, Barbara Warner, Susan Rosenzweig, Deanna Hughes, Alli McHenry Nevin, Daisy, and Queen Kong all propelled this missal. Also my parents are responsible for encouraging my movie habit. My thanks to all concerned.

Introduction: Challenges, Themes, and Solutions

>There are two kinds of people, those who finish what they start and so on.
>—Robert Byrne

My hope is that this book will be both entertaining and provocative. Life stages can be both challenging and perplexing; yet can be enjoyed and understood through cinema (and its animated form of literature). Movies portray puzzles, joys, sorrows, and solutions in ways more vivid than conventional or scholarly writing. Being a clinical psychologist and teaching health professionals for more than two decades has made it clear to me that nothing substitutes for experience. There is no substitute for getting to know people, couples, families, and cultures in live settings. There is no substitute for the satisfying experience of helping people through difficult times as friends, family, or professional caregivers. Furthermore, sharing insights gained from watching, feeling, and recognizing someone else's conundrum (from the comfortable distance of the camera lens) is a powerful and energizing way to learn. Movies, viewed and discussed together get the juices flowing like no journal article ever written. Cinema and theater can provoke a depth of feeling that rivals life, yet they offer enough distance and perspective to ponder new insights and strategies. Seeing the self-defeating or redeeming things people do helps us discover our blind spots and find solutions. The vivid emotionality of movies offers a range of benefits from empathy and anger to laughter and redemption.

When we are stressed and the most pressured, we tend to be the least creative. Hobart Mowrer, a former president of the American Psychological Association, developed the concept of the "neurotic paradox." This refers to a universal principle. Stress, conflict, or panic (especially in situations we handled poorly before) can cause us to repeat ingrained self-defeating patterns. We know logically these reactions are wrong. However, urgency and stress, without fresh options or new perspective, can cause us to repeat bad habits. Willa Cather suggested: "There are only two or three human stories, and they go on repeating themselves as fiercely as if they had never happened before."

Movies can give us the humor, pathos, recognition, enjoyment and perspective to imagine, understand, and then create better beginnings, better stories, and better endings. Movies also beat the idea of only learning about humanity through dry scholarly writing. Emotional learning has logical, contextual, and emotional components. Stress can launch self-defeating patterns or cause us to panic and block the path to creative living. Cinema can give us a new perspective or a new appreciation of emotions and relations. Movies dramatize great examples of unique or universal life puzzles and sometimes life solutions. They can make us happy, puzzled, sad, dumb, or wise. With a distance or perspective, life's dramas, tragedies, and comedies may make more sense.

William James observed that...we learn to swim in the wie helpful idea is that a person, family, or culture's identity is a life-long process of creating, living, telling, and revising life stories. Another lyrical analogy is one developed by the noted child psychologist Bruno Bettelheim, who wrote the book *The Uses of Enchantment: The Meaning and Importance of Fairy Tales*. This book won the National Book Critics Circle Award in 1977. Bettelhiem was born in Vienna in 1903 and received his doctorate from the University of Vienna. He came to America in 1939 after a year in the concentration camps of Dachau and Buchenwald. He was a Distinguished Professor of Education and Professor of Psychology and Psychiatry at the University of Chicago. His other works include *Children of the Dream, Freud and Man's Soul, Love Is Not Enough*, and *The Informed Heart*.

Bettelheim's works elucidate universal dilemmas, and offer us the hope of informed solutions. These contributions complement well the various works of Joseph Campbell (1988) and Carl Jung (1984) on archetypes and universal themes that plague and redeem humanity. A more recent book, *The Writer's Journey* (Vogler, 1998), elaborates how movies or dreams work to create recognition, fascination, pathos, humor, and enjoyment through universal and cross-cultural wisdom. Many other resources are included herein to make the journey entertaining as well as helpful. Understanding universal principles can set the stage for using movies to entertain, learn, relearn, and enjoy the lives we're given. In addition, it is a relatively painless way to learn the essential elements in understanding the hopes and fears that guide people's lives. Chapter 7 goes into more detail about how to discern these motivations. Cinema is a grand medium and a unique perspective to recognize "what's really going on." A number of vantage points are considered that examine classic and unique developmental, relational and personal challenges.

> O wad some Pow'r the giftie gie us
> To see oursels as others see us.
> It wad frae money a blunder free us,
> And foolish notion.
> —Robert Burns

There is a range of universal themes in drama, art, and cinema. Polti (1977) tried to capture them in his book: *The Thirty-Six Dramatic Situations*. There are also predictable stages in life, family, culture, and gender development. These themes are described by Erikson (1980, 1982), Loevinger (1976) and Gilligan (1982). Levinson also described the *Seasons of a Man's Life* (1978), and *Seasons of a Woman's Life* (1995) in works with those titles, respectively. Pittman (1989) has described men, intimacy, and its betrayal. And Scarf (1987) lends great insight into the life of couples as well.

Art, science, religion, and psychotherapy share a goal—to say or do a thing more clearly and honestly than it has been said or done before. The result advances knowledge, freedom, health, and joy.

There are understandable complementary processes in creativity, relationships, and growth through life. Some of these dimensions, such as

form and passion
immersion and emergence
assimilation and accommodation
stabilization and change
integration and reformation
opening and closing

are described by Rollo May (*The Courage to Create*, 1975) and other writers we will consider throughout the book. These processes blend well with what psychology knows about predictable stages of one's life. Life phases complement the core of creative works of art, literature, and the heart of lasting relationships. When a commitment exists, therapy can help reshape relationships so that there is renewal and room for each person to grow. Looking at the "family of origin" history of each person also enlightens the expectations, hopes and fears that people bring into their own intimate relations.

These concepts of creativity, loss, and renewal can enliven therapy when a couple or family understands the predictable stages and the "hopes and fears" in a non-threatening or normalizing atmosphere. It has been said that "what the patient needs is an experience, not an explanation." We will suggest, in a later chapter on therapy, how that might work. Movies convey vicarious experiences. We may choose to understand the experiences later; without the pressure.

Also there is a principle worth mentioning that I learned from a friend and colleague. Jack was a practicing dermatologist, before he retrained as a psychiatrist. He was a kind, concerned, and gifted individual who actually worked as a missionary physician before tackling psychiatry. His insightful sense of humor enhanced his healing gifts.

While we worked together at a psychiatric teaching hospital,
Jack would often humorously suggest that the most important principles in psychiatry were "just like dermatology." After I puzzled over that, he explained, "In dermatology if someone has an open wound what you need to do is clean it, treat it, and do what's necessary to close it. Then you create an environment that ensures healing. On the other hand, if the problem is a closed infection, you have to examine it, open and treat it. Then you must ensure that

the patient avoids the same germs, trauma or foreign insults in the future." After the acute treatment, there is a reintegration of sorts. This reintegration must consider how the insult happened, how to prevent it, or how to avoid or deal with it (if it cannot be avoided) in the future.

This analogy captures what has been called the *minimal interference principle*. Treat what must be treated, but build on strengths and return to the patient's own growth and healing resources. Focusing on existing resources still requires getting to know the patient, his prior strengths, and the extent of demoralization he has sustained. Minimal interference requires knowing the nature and degree of the demoralization sustained. Then the therapist must draw on past strengths after the impediments are removed, and get the patient back on track when his healing resources are reclaimed. Where is Jack when we need him?

THE CRY FOR MYTH

A myth is a way of making sense in a senseless world. Myths are narrative patterns that give significance to our existence (May, 1991). Myths are like the beams in a house: unexposed to outside view, they are the structure that holds the house together so we can live in it.

Creativity, relationships, and growth all involve a balance of form and passion. The goal is to live, understand, convey, or explain something more clearly and honestly than its been experienced or known before (May, 1975; Rybash, Hooyer, & Roodin, 1986). The foundation for creativity in art, literature, and human growth draws on the complementary processes of form and passion. Sincere commitment to the process or relationship is also a driving and renewing force. Rollo May (1991) gave an interesting example of this in his essay, "Peer Gynt: A Man's Problem in Loving". We will revisit this principle often as applied to therapy.

Movies may also be like folktales from different cultures. If so, their archetypal value offers classic and enduring guidance through entertainment and perspective. Alan Chinen (1989) has described how the folk stories of different countries and people reflect attitudes and traditions about the second half of life. Elders are highly valued in many countries, but less often in America. Chinen's observations elaborate the life story variations in different countries.

Joseph Campbell (1988) did much to help us understand culture, archetype, and the process of change. He relied on Jungian tenets and cross-cultural (universal) processes. The symbols of every culture define growth, adversity, and change. Vogler (1998) wrote the book, *The Writer's Journey: Mythic Structure*, on the similarities of effective movie plots and these universal themes and processes. He drew heavily from Campbell and also Bruno Bettelheim.

Introduction 5

> By reaching out of psychology and into literature with an eye to common sense and plain language, we aim to loosen the soil that has buried the story of (human) experience, removing the thatch of a mystifying language in order to see what grows.
> —Bruno Bettelheim, *The Uses of Enchantment*

> His life had been confused and disordered....but if he could once return to a certain starting place and go over it all slowly, he could find what that thing was.
> —F. Scott Fitzgerald, *The Great Gatsby and the American Dream*

> All sorrows can be borne if you put them in a story or tell a story about them.
> —Isak Dinesen (Karen Blixen), 1885–1962

One goal of this book is to look for enduring human strengths, weaknesses, and patterns of change and growth. Pursuing enduring patterns and processes is the substance of both art and human growth. An entertaining model to start with is a book on the patterns we live and the roles we play in love, sex, and marriage. We will consider a number of such models throughout the book.

There is an entertaining yet wise example of the phases of romantic love and its vicissitudes through three predictable stages. Goldstine et al. (1977) wrote an entertaining yet wise book, *The Dance Away Lover*. We can borrow these styles and preview a "good fit" to various movies along the way. Some capstone descriptions of people's style in relations include the following:

   The Dance Away Lover
   The Anxious Ingenue
   The Disarmer
   The Provider
   The Prizewinner
   The Fragile
   The Pleaser
   The Victim
   The Ragabash
   The Tough-Fragile

The roles are shiftable and interactive. The styles also can predict what kind of person is attracted to what style or qualities in others. Recognizing that there are (more or less) three stages of relationships offers insight into the tasks, outlooks, and opportunities for change and new beginnings once the initial glow starts to pale.

STAGE I: FALLING IN LOVE

Stage I is the "Ga-Ga" stage when love or lust eclipses reason. Add sex and romance and stir. This stage is the focus of much of our popular music. The reader can come up with many examples. Prime the pump.

STAGE II: REALITIES OF RELATIONS

Realities, disappointments, conflicts, failures, letdowns, and rough waters can all be forerunners of growth with some appreciation of interpersonal valence and the models of intimacy and maturity we carry. The qualities that attract us to each other often become the qualities that irritate us most.

A frequent example from therapy is when the therapist asks a couple, "What attracted you to each other in the first place?"

One common answer might be a woman's reflection, "He was so much fun, and spur-of-the-moment, off-the-cuff and unpredictable. There was never a dull moment!" While the guy's answer about his beau goes like this: "She was someone I knew I could always count on. She was focused, sensible, always able to put things in perspective."

Then, when asked, "What are the problems now?" it is common to hear about a "reversal." The example from the same couple would go like this: "He's irresponsible about money, never on time and doesn't know when to get serious". He complains…that we never have any fun! Everything has to be planned and what do we have to look forward to?" Without the understanding that these times of conflict can signal a time for growth and redefining the relationship, hard times will ensue.

That giddy initial attraction of Stage I can give way to Stage II, which is marked by alienation, pessimism, and resentment. Plus, we can project our foibles, fears, and bad qualities onto the other person. This second stage is the focus of a large part of the blues or country and western music (e.g., "my baby done me wrong," or "feeling single and seein' double." The reader may think of examples here as well. Stage II can be a threat when the initial heady romantic projections lose luster, and we discover the realities of day-to-day living. Or this stage can be a spur to accept our own foibles and redefine the relation after the glow of glistening bliss subsides.

The concept of *reversal* is crucial here. Reversal is a variation on the Jungian theme of projection, and each person's male and female qualities (anima/animus) and processes. The qualities that attract us to another at first, often become the qualities that irritate and breed blame and conflict. New diversions, affairs, or distancing can follow.

Later in the book we quote a family therapist, Gus Napier, who discovered that in every relationship each person is trying to "grow the other one up." By that he means that we want to train or change our mate to "better meet our own needs." This truth is important when dealing with Stage II, because its universality can be used to laugh at the conflict and address it with collaboration rather than conflict.

STAGE III: RENEWAL, CARING, AND COMMITMENT

This stage of a relationship represents the opportunity to grow by creating, preserving, renewing, or redefining a commitment or relation. Relations can become stale or problematic, or the relationship can mature and renew via redefining and rebalancing each person's style, as well as his/her investment or commitment to the relation.

The *Dance Away Lover* is an entertaining resource on interpersonal style, expectations in relations, and unwitting motivations.

Jay Haley, in his books, *Strategies of Psychotherapy* (1990) and *The Power Tactics of Jesus Christ* (1986), also describes some essential patterns in human relations. Haley suggests that in any relation, two people struggle for control in defining the relationship. There are "power" motives that may contend with the wish for closeness or intimacy. There are verbal and nonverbal strategies to gain parity in a relation. The strategies can be unwitting (driven by a person's style or motivations) as well as intentional. The curse of insight described earlier works well with Haley's strategies.

Haley comes from the communication theory tradition, which counts Gregory Bateson, Donald Jackson, John Weakland, Paul Watzlawick, and Virginia Satir among its founders. Their varied works are important in understanding interpersonal style, relations, motivations, and capacity for intimacy.

Some of the essential human ways (secrets?) to strengthen improve, or foil relationships are intentional and some are habitual. Think about that for a moment. When doing therapy, I usually give a patient the benefit of the doubt when together we discover some self-defeating pattern. If the therapy relationship is solid, the offending pattern or motivation can be identified. Logic would suggest that the patient would then change his ways. However, people may be unaware of their interpersonal impact or even their motives.

What the therapist can do is give the patient, the "curse of insight." However, pointing out a self-defeating pattern or behavior doesn't always change it. Relationships are often defined by what people do not talk about as much as what they do discuss. However, naming the pattern or interpersonal style makes the unconscious...conscious! And the patient can no longer plead ignorance. Like any creative process, relations are a balance of form (interpersonal style) and passion (fervor).

Psychoanalyst Elio Frattaroli (2001), in his book, *Healing the Soul in the Age of the Brain*, suggests that symptoms are sometimes good for the soul. Symptoms can spur us to consider our bias and discover which beliefs, hopes, and fears help us and which may actually complicate or hinder our lives.

A pair of wise women, Peske and West (1999) in their creative book, *Cinematherapy: The Girl's Guide to Movies for Every Mood,* describe movies as, "more than entertainment: they're self-medication!" Then their book catalogues and pinpoints timeless themes, dreams and anxieties through "movies as prescriptions for laughter, growth and entertaining insight."

8 Cinema and Life Development

Many valuable sources are suggested throughout our book to complement the fun of using movies to train therapists and heal lives across the life span. Stories in cinema can help us understand the dreams, hopes, and fears that impel or impede people's lives.

REFERENCES

Bettelheim, Bruno (1977). *The uses of enchantment: The meaning and importance of fairy tales.* New York: Vintage Books.

Black, Evan Imber and Roberts, Janine (1993). *Rituals for our times: Celebrating, healing and changing our lives and our relationships.* New York: HarperPerennial.

Campbell, Joseph (1988). *The power of myth.* New York: Doubleday.

Carlsen, Mary Baird (1991). *Creative aging: A meaning-making perspective.* New York: Norton.

Chinen, A. B. (1989). *In the everafter: Fairy tales for the second half of life.* Willmette, ILL: Chiron Publishers.

Coles, Robert (1989). *The call of stories: Teaching and the moral imagination.* Boston: Houghton Mifflin.

Cousineau, Phillip & Brown, Phillip (eds.) (1990). *Joseph Campbell on his life and work.* New York: Harper & Row.

Doniger O'Flaherty, Wendy (1995). *Other people's myths: The cave of echoes.* Chicago: University of Chicago Press.

Erikson, Erik (1980). *Identity and the life cycle.* New York: Norton.

Erikson, Erik (1982). *The life cycle completed.* New York: Norton.

Fowler, J. W. (1981). *Stages of faith.* San Francisco: Harper & Row.

Frank, Jerome and Frank, Julia (1991). *Persuasion and healing: A comparative Study of psychotherapy* 3rd ed. Baltimore: Johns Hopkins University Press.

Frattaroli, Elio (2001). *Healing the soul in the age of the brain.* New York: Viking.

Gabbard, G. O. (ed.) (2001). *Psychoanalysis and film.* New York: Karnac.

Gilligan, C. (1982). *In a different voice: Psychological theory and women's development.* Cambridge, MA: Harvard University Press.

Goldstine, Daniel, Larner, Katherine, Zuckerman, Shirley & Goldstine, Hillary (1977). The dance away lover: And other roles we play in love, sex and marriage. New York: Ballantine.

Gordon, David (1978). *Therapeutic metaphors.* Cupertino, CA: META Publications.

Gutmann, D. (1987). *Reclaimed powers: Toward a new psychology of men and women in later life.* New York: Basic Books.

Haley, Jay (1986). *The power tactics of jesus christ and other essays,* 2nd ed. Rockville, MD: The Triangle Press. Distributed by Norton, New York.

Haley, Jay (1990). *Strategies of psychotherapy,* 2nd ed. Rockville, MD: Triangle Press. Distributed by Norton: New York.

Hudson-O'Hanlon, P. O. and O'Hanlon-Hudson, H. O. (1993). *Rewriting love stories: Brief marital therapy.* New York: Norton.

Josselson, Ruthellen (1996). *Revising herself: The story of women's life from college to midlife.* Oxford: Oxford University Press.
Jung, C. (1984). *Dream analysis.* Princeton, NJ: Princeton University Press.
Lerner, Harriett (1997a). *The dance of deception.* New York: HarperTrade.
Lerner, Harriett (1997b). *The dance of intimacy.* New York: HarperTrade.
Lerner, Harriett (1999). *The dance of anger.* New York: HarperTrade.
Levinson, D. J. (1978). *The seasons of a man's life.* New York: Knopf.
Levinson, D. J. (1995). *The seasons of a woman's life.* New York: Knopf.
Levinson, D. J. (1986). A conception of adult development. *American Psychologist, 41*, 3–14.
Linn, Matthew, Fabricant, Sheila and Linn, Dennis (1988). *Healing the eight stages of life.* New York: Paulist Press.
Loevinger, J. (1976). *Ego development.* San Francisco: Jossey-Bass.
May, Rollo (1975). *The courage to create.* New York: Norton.
May, Rollo (1991). *The cry for myth.* New York: Delta Publishing.
May, Rollo (1969). *Love and will.* New York: Dell.
McAdams, D. P. (1997). *The stories we live by: Personal myths and the making of the self.* New York: Guilford.
Peske, Nancy and West, Beverly (1999). *Cinematherapy: The girl's guide to movies for every mood.* New York: Dell.
Pittman, Frank (1989). *Private lives: Infidelity and the betrayal of intimacy.* New York: Norton.
Polti, Georges (1977). Translated by L. Ray. *The thirty-six dramatic situations.* Boston: The Writer, Inc.
Rybash, J., Hoyer, W. and Roodin, P. (1986). *Adult cognition and aging: Developmental changes in processing, knowing and thinking.* New York: Pergamon.
Satir, Virginia (1988). *The new peoplemaking.* Mountain View, CA: Science and Behavioral Books.
Scarf, Maggie (1987). *Intimate partners: Patterns in love and marriage.* New York: Ballantine.
Thompson, E. H. (1994). *Older men's lives.* Thousand Oaks, CA: Sage.
Vaillant, George (1977). *Adaptation to life.* Boston: Little, Brown & Company.
Vogler, C. V. (1998). *The writer's journey: Mythic structure for writers.* Studio City, CA: M. Wiese Productions.
Wedding, D. and Boyd, M. (1999). *Movies and mental illness: Using films to understand psychopathology.* New York: McGraw-Hill.
White, M. and Epston, D. (1990). *Narrative means to therapeutic ends.* New York: Norton.
Zinsser, William (ed). (1988). *Spiritual quests: The art and craft of religious writing.* Boston: Houghton Mifflin.

1
Life Span Development: Cornerstones and Scaffolding

Life moves in cycles filled with transition, change, and integration. Sometimes the process is gradual and almost imperceptible. Life brings us closer to joy or long-sought goals, yet sometimes to the brink of despair. Most theories of development suggest that strength comes from navigating life challenges, creating hope, and developing resilience. In this chapter we consider the notion of *leitmotifs* or life bets that may guide us and give us insight about ourselves and others' motivations. Motivations range from high-minded and joyful ones, in good times, through reactive perspectives in tough times, and even extremes of desperation when one's very survival seems at stake.

Erik Erikson (1980, 1982) has given us a marvelous legacy to understand the challenges and possibilities of each person's life span. And many others (Gilligan, Ward, & Taylor, 1981; Kohlberg & Gilligan, 1971; Fowler. 1981; Bowen, 1978; Kerr & Bowen, 1988), to name a few, help us understand variations on Erikson's discoveries.

Healthy Outcomes of Erikson's Stages

Hope	Trust vs. Mistrust
Will	Autonomy vs. Shame, Doubt
Purpose	Initiative vs. Guilt
Competence	Industry vs. Inferiority
*Fidelity	Identity vs. Identity Diffusion
*Love	Intimacy vs. Isolation
*Care	Generativity vs. Stagnation
*Wisdom	Integrity vs. Despair

* Adult Years

12   Cinema and Life Development

> Pray that your loneliness may spur you into finding something to live for, great enough to die for.
> —Swedish Diaries 1951

> The seasons have changed, and the light, the weather and the hour. But it is the same land. And I begin to know the map, and to get my bearings.
> —Dag Hammarskjold (1905–1961), Swedish diplomat, United Nations, shortly before his death

Sometimes the life stage model is misunderstood. The Erikson model is not a "pass or fail," kind of exam. A more reasonable understanding is that emotional strength is a continuum or a ratio. One psychologist (Hawley, 1988) has even developed a format to anchor people's relative psychosocial resilience or strength. Hawley's instrument allows quantification of a person's relative resolution or progress along Erikson's universal path. This psychological questionnaire yields a ratio of relative success along the eight stages. Movies are generally more fun, however, than psychology tests.

One of the things we want to do in this chapter is highlight cinema and examples to anchor and show relative emotional strength. We will try to do this considering people or families who span the spectrum from overwhelmed (or diffuse), foreclosed (protectively rigid), in-transition, or active change (moratorium), to the successful integration of a mature (achieved) identity. Such success is the product of tried-and-true ways to overcome, cope, and integrate creative ways to relate. This personal and interpersonal strength comes from facing challenges, adversity, opportunities and thereby succeeding in emotional and interpersonal health. Movies provide endless options to make this learning or growth provocative, troubling, enlightening, and even enjoyable.

CORNERSTONES

Core dynamics, *lietmotifs*, life hunches, life bets, guiding motives, developmental stages, and cross-generational differences are some of the processes that help us understand growth across the life span. Concepts that can serve as road markers on the journey to psychological health include the following:

> pathology vs. healthy responding,
> coping styles that do and don't work,
> stages of relationships, and
> cultural and gender differences.

Learning the terrain gives us clues to therapeutic relationships and strategies. Another guiding perspective suggests "some things are too important to be taken seriously." This principle often helps take some of the pressure off the patient or the therapist. The task of therapy usually requires a new perspective. The pressure that attends the serious task is helped by humor. Metaphor and analogies can prompt creative solutions. A good understanding or conceptualization sometimes can be translated into memorable quips or sayings. One example might be a person who is very hard on himself, by being critical and self-punitive. He has done it so long, it is automatic and interferes with healing or growth. "I need to stop shoulding (also known as "shitting" or berating) on myself. The word play and hyperbola can be used to recognize and eventually change a self-defeating pattern.

A *case conceptualization* is an understanding of a person's motivations, fears, and resources. A good understanding provides a collaborative plan for treatment and healing. This important process is revisited throughout the book (especially Chapter 7).

PREVIEWS OF A FEW ARCHETYPAL MOVIE EXAMPLES: SCAFFOLDING AND REBUILDING

> We make progress by a constant spiraling back and forth between the inner world and the outer one, the personal and the political, the self and the circumstances. Nature doesn't move in a straight line, and as part of nature, neither do we.
> —Gloria Steinem

What can movies show us to better understand the experiences, beliefs, and strategies on which we bet our lives? The possibilities are endless, but we can help the search by highlighting a few classic examples. Through movies we can understand people—what created them, what sustains them, when they need change, and what strategies they need to survive and grow. Practicing on movies is fun and powerful. They are marvelous because films create an emotional level that rivals real life, plus they give us the distance and perspective to be creative. These same qualities can be used to train therapists in a wide range of pressures, possibilities, and understanding.

Earlier we suggested that creativity is a balance of form and passion (May, 1977). The principle also applies to creating lives and relationships, and eventually revitalizing them. Often when we need to be the most creative we are the least creative. This paradox happens because pressures can make us temporarily ineffective or "dumb." We grow by navigating these challenges; then perspective and experience may help produce creative solutions in art and in life. Emotional resilience or perspective may come from difficult times.

We have organized the life stage challenges using Erikson's (1980, 1982) format, while suggesting movies that capture the issues and possibilities that accompany these ages. I have chosen at least one film in each stage as an example, and then list others with those themes. Asking people to add their own favorites has been a fun and effective exercise when teaching courses on psychodiagnosis and psychotherapy.

14   Cinema and Life Development

BASIC TRUST VERSUS. MISTRUST: HOPE

On the essential trustfulness of others as the well as fundamental sense of one's own trustworthiness.

After Hours (1986).
Rosanna Arquette, Griffin Dunne, Teri Garr
This is an edgy black comedy with twists and turns of adults struggling with whom they can trust. The movie has been described as similar to the "*Blue Velvet*" genre with the addition of Catholicism.

Black Stallion (1979)
Kelly Reno, Mickey Rooney, Teri Garr
A young boy and a wild Arabian Stallion form a deep relationship after surviving a ship tragedy. Trust can be cross species as well as between people.

Look Who's Talking (1989)
Kirstie Alley, John Travolta.
Alley's character becomes pregnant and the father of the baby deserts her. While in labor, she takes a cab to the hospital where she meets Travolta (the driver). Much of the movie is seen through the eyes of the new baby, Mikey. Alley searches for a father for her baby and eventually comes to love Travolta.
Developmental Theme: "Mikey" learns that his needs can be satisfied by his mother and his babysitter. Several scenes practically spell out the themes of the stage. There is also an overriding love story between the actors. This can be seen in Intimacy versus Isolation as Alley's character is getting older and more concerned about spending her life alone. The movie is simple and cute and probably one of a very few that actually covers this stage while it is occurring.

Of Mice and Men (1939)
Lon Chaney, Jr., Burgess Meredith, Betty Field.
A powerful adaptation of Steinbeck's tragedy about the friendship between two itinerant Southern ranch hands during the Great Depression. Chaney is wonderful as the mentally retarded gentle giant. He is cared for by the migrant worker, Meredith. They find themselves in an irreversible situation when a woman is accidentally killed. The film earned Academy Award nominations for best picture and best score.
Developmental Theme: Their friendship captures the essence of trust and hope even in the face of tragedy. A heart-wrenching, but enduring example of caring and human qualities that are eternal.

AUTONOMY VERSUS SHAME/DOUBT:WILL

A clash of wills between parents and child.

Mask (1985)
Cher, Sam Elliot, Laura Dern
A young boy disfigured by the disease elephantiasis struggles with his identity, worth, and his capacity to love and be loved.

1984 (1984)
John Hurt, Richard Burton, Cyril Cusack.
Based on George Orwell's classic book, the movie tackles the tension between individual freedom and social responsibility.

King of Hearts (1966)
Alan Bates, Genevieve Bujold
Set in World War I, a soldier wanders into a war-torn village and finds that lunatics from the local asylum have escaped and are the only one's left in the village. They want to make the soldier their king. After making many discoveries about this new so-called freedom, they decide the asylum is better than the outside world.

Look Who's Talking, Too! (1990)
Kirstie Alley, John Travolta.
A sequel to the first. At this point Travolta's character has married Alley's character. The two soon find out that they are expecting another child. Much of the film is seen through the eyes of the now-two-year-old Mikey. After the birth of his little sister, she too shares her views of what's going on. Mikey is trying to be a good older brother while contending with his own toilet training. The sister is learning about trust and warmth. Conflict arises when the parents constantly disagree and eventually separate. By the movie's ending, Mikey learns some self-sufficiency and the parents reunite.
Developmental Theme: Mikey progresses and his sister is beginning to master feeding and walking. Both children are good examples of age expected Autonomy by the movie's end. Some people may tire of the storyline, but it highlights the issues in a playful fashion.

Stand By Me (1986)
River Phoenix, Corey Feldman, Keifer Sutherland, Richard Dreyfus.
An adaptation of Stephen King's short story "The Body." This is a sentimental story of four 12-year-old friends trekking into the Oregon wilderness to find the body of a missing boy. They learn about death, friendship, and courage, thereby moving toward autonomy. Rob Reiner directs this memorable experience.
Developmental Theme: Captures the concept of developing and guiding one's will as the parents' or society's rules become more complicated.

INITIATIVE VERSUS GUILT: PURPOSE

Child's identification with his parents or society, seen as big, powerful and intrusive.

> *An Officer and a Gentleman* (1982)
> *Ordinary People* (1980)
> *To Kill a Mockingbird* (1962)

Home Alone (1990)
Macaulay Culkin, Joe Pesci.
A large extended family plans to visit Paris for the Christmas holiday. In the hustle of leaving for the airport, the youngest son (Culkin) is accidentally left home alone. The story involves the young boy surviving on his own while his mother tries to get back to him. While alone he takes care of things perfectly and even manages to fight off two burglars in a funny series of events. Eventually the family returns, and he realizes how much he loved and missed them.

One Flew Over the Cuckoo's Nest (1975)
Danny DeVito, Christopher Lloyd, Jack Nicholson, Brad Dourif, Louise Fletcher.
While not age-appropriate to this developmental stage, the characters in this Oregon looney bin are struggling with guilt and initiative. These issues haunt the patients and staff. Humor and pathos mix in a memorable psychiatric society.
In a way this film (and the book that inspired it) also captures adolescent themes of rebelling against authority figures that marked the later stages of the Vietnam era.
Developmental Theme: Adolescence often recapitulates this earlier developmental stage.

INDUSTRY VERSUS INFERIORITY: COMPETENCE

I am what I learn.

> *Places in the Heart* (1984)
> *Taxi Driver* (1976)
> *The Verdict* (1982)
> *Five Easy Pieces* (1970)
> *Out of Africa* (1985)
> *A Thousand Clowns* (1965)

Curly Sue (1991)
>James Belushi, Kelly Lynch.
>Bill and little Curley Sue are homeless travelers trying to survive by swindling and/or charming others. They travel because they are afraid that a child protection agency will catch up with them and take Sue, and they will be separated. They fake a car accident to get a meal and meet a beautiful attorney in the process. The attorney takes them in, falls in love with the little girl, and by movie's end, they become a family. An additional theme is the love that develops between the adults: intimacy versus isolation.

The Verdict (1982)
>Paul Newman, James Mason, Charlotte Rampling.
>Newman is an alcoholic failed attorney reduced to ambulance chasing. A friend gives him an apparently easy malpractice case that turns out to be his last chance at redeeming his career and his life. Powerful performances abound as Newman's character is not the only one looking for redemption or a sense of purpose and worth.
>*Developmental Theme*: What have I learned and what is my worth?

IDENTITY AND REPUDIATION VS. IDENTITY DIFFUSION: FIDELITY

>Integrate prior identifications into a more complete identity.

To be or not to be.

>*The Breakfast Club* (1985)
>*Risky Business* (1983)
>*St. Elmo's Fire* (1985)
>*Easy Rider* (1969)

We're No Angels (1989)
>Robert DeNiro, Sean Penn, Hoyt Axton.
>In 1935 De Niro's and Penn's characters are prisoners accidentally caught up in a prison escape. In order to avoid capture, they pose as priests in a monastery near the Canadian border. While De Niro plots different ways to cross the border without being caught, Penn discovers that he enjoys the life of a priest. He also discovers who he really is and when the opportunity to escape arises, he cannot leave.

A River Runs Through It (1992)
>Craig Sheffer, Brad Pitt, Tom Skerritt.
>A thoughtful exploration of family ties and coming of age. A finely crafted tale set in Montana during the early part of the century. A Presbyterian minister teaches his two sons (one troubled and one on his way to success)

about life and religion through the metaphor of fly-fishing. Based on the novel by Norman Maclean.
Developmental Theme: Possibilities, risks, and personal fidelity.

INTIMACY AND SOLIDARITY VERSUS ISOLATION: LOVE

Successful passage through adolescence breeds an ability to be intimate with others.

Alfie (1966)
About Last Night (1986)
The Big Chill (1983)
The Cemetery Club (1993)
The Graduate (1969)
An Officer and a Gentleman (1982)
Annie Hall (1977)
Harold and Maude (1971)
Who's Afraid of Virginia Woolf (1966)
Falling in Love (1984)
Deep Throat (1973)
Shampoo (1975)

Shirley Valentine (1989)
Pauline Collins, Tom Conti, Alison Steadman.
A lively middle-aged English housewife gets a new lease on life when she travels to Greece without her husband. Collins reprises her London and Broadway stage triumph. Her character frequently addresses the audience to explain her thoughts and feelings. (This stream of consciousness is also a powerful technique in Woody Allen's *Annie Hall*, and a great tool for training psychotherapists). Collins energy and vitality are inspiring. She captured the British Academy Award for best actress.

Housesitter (1992)
Goldie Hawn, Steve Martin, Dana Delaney
Martin's character, Newton, has just proposed to his longtime girlfriend (Delaney), and gives her a new house he built in their hometown.
She refuses both. Crushed, he goes back to the city and meets Gwen (Goldie Hawn). He tells her about the beautiful home and what has happened. He goes back to his life in the city, but unbeknownst to him she moves out to the empty house in the town. Gwen convinces the town, and even his parents, that she is his wife. They all fall in love with her. When he returns to the home, he is trapped in this elaborate scheme, but agrees to go along in hopes of making the old girlfriend jealous. A good comedy ensues. At the end Newton realizes that it is Gwen that he loves and the two commit to each other.
Developmental Theme: Us (or me) against them.

GENERATIVITY VERSUS. STAGNATION AND SELF-ABSORPTION

Interest in establishing and guiding the next generation via children and/or creative, productive endeavors.

Cross Creek (1983)
Educating Rita (1983)
The Hospital (1971)
Places in the Heart (1984)
Sophie's Choice (1982)
Hannah and Her Sisters (1986)
Middle Age Crazy (1980)
The Natural (1984)
Twice in a Lifetime (1985)
The Verdict (1982)
Nobody's Fool (1994)
Tender Mercies (1983)
An Unmarried Woman (1978)
The Stone Boy (1984)
Fried Green Tomatoes (1991)
A Woman's Tale (Australia) (1992)
Strangers in Good Company (Canada) (1991)
Dreamchild (Britain) (1985)
Unforgiven (1992)
Used People (1992)
Wrestling Ernest Hemingway (1993)
The Swimmer (1968)

City Slickers (1991)
Billy Crystal, Daniel Stern, Bruno Kirby, Jack Palance.
Three couples often take vacations together. This year the men decide to go together on a cattle-driving encounter across the plains. They expected nothing more than a good time. However, the older trail boss (Palance) demands much from them, and even frightens them initially. They consider giving up, but continue. The three friends discuss their lots in life and their respective crises. Palance's character is the strange crusty mentor who creates the conditions for the younger men struggling with ruined commitments and other issues to reconsider and forge anew. He shares his unique secret for life.

Fried Green Tomatoes (1991)
Kathy Bates, Jessica Tandy, Mary Stuart Masterson.
Two stories about: four women, love, friendship, Southern charm, and eccentricity. Set in contemporary Alabama with many flashbacks to childhood memories from a feisty woman in a retirement home. Tandy is a wise lady and Bates is the 30–40-something woman awash in identity confusion and hilarity. The two women create a bond that enlightens and energizes both their

lives. Words don't adequately capture the texture, humor, and themes portrayed in this movie. Erik Erikson would be pleased with such a clear human example of his stages. Erikson probably would have laughed and cried with the rest of us in the audience.

When using this film in graduate psychology courses, the students have uniformly learned to grasp the full meaning of the developmental stages in immediacy and in the posterity.

Developmental Theme: Who am I? What have I been, and who can I still become?

INTEGRITY VERSUS REGRET OR DESPAIR

What has happened, what has been learned and what has been given over a lifetime? Accepting shortcomings and limitations while giving to a larger history. Understanding what is lasting by integrating the reality of a lifetime. Can include life review and the "end game." Builds on all the other stages and healthy stories from life's loves, tragedies and labors. An opportunity to put things in perspective and pass along the joys, dangers and secrets of the journey. Recognizing and conveying those values and relations that live beyond one's own life.

> *Cocoon* (1985)
> *A Very Old Man with Enormous Wings* (Cuba) (1988)
> *The Gin Game* (1984)
> *On Golden Pond* (1981)
> *Terms of Endearment* (1983)
> *Resurrection* re: healing (1980)
> *Trip to Bountiful* (1985)
> *Shadowbox* re: hospice (1980)
> *Harold and Maude* (1971)
> *The Last of His Tribe* (1992)
> *A Walk in the Clouds* (1995)
> *Steel Magnolias* (1989)
> *A Gathering of Old Men* (1992)
> *To Dance with the White Dog* (1993)
> *Age Old Friends* (1989)
> *Wild Strawberries* (Sweden) (1957)
> *King Lear* (Paul Schofield version (1971)
> *Old Gringo* (1989)
> *Diary of a Mad Old Man* (1988)
> *The Ballad of Narayama* (Japan) (1983)

That's Life (1986)
 Jack Lemmon, Julie Andrews.
As Lemmon's character turns sixty he reflects on his life and choices. His wife (Andrews) and his three grown children try to support him as they deal

with their own problems. The movie takes place over a one week's time period. Lemmon does not know that his wife is secretly awaiting the results of a cancer test. The gamut of life problems arises with the family and are faced with various styles. Lemmon gains some sense of perspective, and acceptance. The various family problems are resolved to some degree, and the wife's cancer tests are negative.

A Walk in the Clouds (1995)
Aitana Sanchez-Gijon, Keanu Reeves, Anthony Quinn.

A mystical story that begins as a returning World War II soldier discovers his dull job and unhappy marriage leave him few options. The good-hearted but perplexed man meets a beautiful but pregnant daughter of a possessive Napa Valley vineyard owner. He agrees to pose as her husband, and his life will never be the same. Anthony Quinn is the grandfather and family patriarch, and a repository of wisdom, love, and mystical perspective. A wonderful grape-harvest scene, and a model of wisdom and perspective in the face of countless tragedies ensue. This movie was based on the 1942 Italian film, *Four Steps in the Clouds*.

Developmental Theme: What is lasting in our lives and beyond, and how have I lived?

Creativity, intimacy and human development share a common force or principle. These achievements require a balance of form and passion (May, 1977). In human relationships each person must have his/her own identity, but also find ways to be vulnerable, connected and intimate. The balance (with commitment to the relation) allows passion to energize and be sustained.

In art (of all media) there are periods when a certain structure of expression is preferred. For example, iambic pentameter was the accepted form for poetry in the Elizabethan (or Shakespearean) era. At a later time the verse of e. e. cummings (sic) was more free-form and stretched the boundaries of acceptable grammar and structure. Music has had similar transitions. Consider the beautiful ballads of the 1930s and 1940s, which gave rise to an initial horror at the early forms of jazz or rock music. Impressionist paintings were initially criticized as the coming demise of art. Now the impressionists are often panned as passé by modern artists.

Human development, relationships, and art evolve in a balance of periods of stabilization and periods of change. Understanding that shared process helps make change less of a threat. As therapists, knowing whether the patient needs change or requires stabilization, is an important skill.

In an old Charlie Brown cartoon about baseball, Charlie (as the coach) asks the character Pig Pen, "Well, do you need help with your swing, your stance or your timing?"
Pig Pen responds, "Please...just help me hold the bat!"

Judging the scope of change required, is at least as important as good skills and accurate diagnosis.

The cross-generational issues, biases, pulls, and directives that parents foist upon their progeny can be haunting voices that guide, direct, and befuddle every new generation. Movies can teach us a lot about this dimension.

Various Woody Allen movies are important to mention. The book *Woody Allen on Woody Allen in Conversation with Stig Bjorkman* (1993), considers 24 films by the enigmatic New Yorker. A discussion of Woody Allen should include a caveat. He ain't no role model. Many artists' lives are not pretty things. But the ability to capture universal human themes, and make the variety of human relationships clearer, may not always coincide with being a role model. In the writer's own family, a favorite quote was, "Some people's role in life is to serve as a bad example." But back to Woody's contributions. Any of these could be a springboard for discussion and practice in diagnosis and treatment planning.

> *Take the Money and Run* (first directing excursion)
> *Bananas*
> *Play it Again, Sam*
> *Everything You Wanted to Know About Sex...*
> *Sleeper*
> *A Midsummer Night's Sex Comedy*
> *Annie Hall*
> *Manhattan*
> *Stardust Memories*
> *Crimes and Misdemeanors*
> *Interiors*
> *Broadway Danny Rose*
> *New York Stories*
> *Radio Days*
> *The Purple Rose of Cairo*
> *Another Woman*
> *Alice*
> *New York Stories*
> *Husbands and Wives*
> *Shadows and Fog*
> *Manhattan Murder Mystery*
> *Hannah and Her Sisters*

This last film was one of Allen's serious studies. Not everyone liked him setting comedy aside. In a showing in one Midwestern theater much of the audience, expecting Allen's usual zany humor, were outraged at his foray into serious relational warfare.

The family psychiatrist Murray Bowen (1978) is a great resource who clarified that independence and the ability to really achieve intimacy had much to do with how well we "individuate" from our family of origin. Healthy individuation is the ability to love without unduly guarding against another's influence. On one hand, a person may be "enmeshed" and have little emotional autonomy from the family in which he grew up. On the other hand some people have a forced or reactive "distance" from their family. This apparent independence may actually cause as much trouble as being "enmeshed" when we attempt to create loving relationships in our own generation. Murray and his colleagues suggest that a prognosis for healthy intimacy is predicted by a person's bedrock confidence and facility in being an equal partner in relations. The enduring challenge is to be your own person while also capable of intimacy.

The Story of Us (1999)
   Michelle Pfeiffer and Bruce Willis.
Marriage, divorce, with parental influences depicted hysterically and vividly.

In an unforgettable scene (just after the couple has finished a marriage counseling session) we flash to the couple in bed talking. But also in bed with them are both sets of parents as a surrealistic, irritating, and funny presence. A little bit of the dialogue goes like this:

Key: H (husband); W (wife); H's mom; H's dad; W's mom; W's dad

The Dialogue

Scenario: Wife, husband, and both sets of parents are all sitting in the same bed against the headboard. However only the audience can see the parents.

H: (Laughing as he talks about the marriage counselor). I can't believe that guy charged us for the full session.
W: The man was peeing on our time.
W's mom: All that therapy was just a waste of time and money.
W: When you think about it, where did all that therapy really get us?
H: It got us right here, laughing about it.
W's dad: He's right.
W's mom: Oh what are you talking about? Once it's broken it can never really be fixed.
W: I don't know
W's dad: The Queen has spoken.
W's mom: What?!
W's dad: Nothing.
W: maybe it's just too soon.
H: Too soon? What are you talking about?
H's mom: The whole point of having a knock-down drag-out fight is playing "hide the salami" afterward.
W's dad: See!? (as he looks at his wife)
H's mom: Let hard times bring you together. Nobody said it would be easy.
H: Can't we let hard times bring us together? Nobody said it was going to be easy.

24 Cinema and Life Development

H's dad: It's like the Andrews Sisters after "Boogie Woogie Bugle Boy," and before "Don't Sit Under the Apple Tree..."
W: (incredulously) The Andrews Sisters!?
H: Sure, they didn't stop singing just because they had a few music flops. They hung in there and rest is music history.
H's dad: (Singing) "Don't sit under the apple tree with anyone else but me..."
(H's wife joins in and W's dad snaps along)..."with anyone else but me" (continues singing the rest of the time).
W: Uh, I just don't understand why you're bringing up the Andrews sisters now.
W's Mom: No, no, no! You're singing. These kids are in trouble and you're singing.
H's mom: Oh Dot! Put out once in awhile. Your face won't be so tight.
W's dad: (to H's mom) Slut!
W: I just don't understand what the Andrews Sisters' career slump has to do with our marital problems!?
H: What am I supposed to do? Make our marriage worse by dwelling on every little thing?
W: Is that what you think I do? Is that how you see me?
W's mom: You're a child . . .
W: That I just dwell on everything?
W's mom: A 72-yearr old infant.
W: There are real problems here...that we haven't even begun to deal with.
H: Don't you think I know that? Jesus! What happened to you? What happened to that fun girl? The one with the pith helmet? Where did she go?
W: You don't think I ask myself that every day? You beat her out of me. There's no room for her.
W's mom: You think it's all fun and games, Harry.
H: I guess it's all my fault you hang on to every little thing.
W's mom: A car doesn't drive by itself.
H: It's my fault that you can't let go of anything?
W's mom: Someone has to take the wheel.
H: (to his wife) It's all my fault that you turned into your Goddamn mother?!
W: F___ you!

All the parents disappear, and the wife walks out of the room

  The movie is funnier and more powerful than the written dialogue, but hopefully the main effect is preserved. The family psychiatrist Murray Bowen (1978) would probably give his blessing to this accurate example of swinging from the family tree.

Consider a preview of men's and women's issues. Then we can return in a later chapters to flesh out the details.

Men

Wild Strawberries. (Ingmar Bergman, director.) A landmark film of fantasy, dreams and nightmares about an aging professor coming to terms with anxieties and guilt.
Stand by Me. (Rob Reiner, director) Pre-adolescence, friendship and death in a small town.
A River Runs Through It. (Robert Redford, director) Family ties and coming of age in Montana.
Age Old Friends. (Hume Cronyn and Jessica Tandy) The struggle with aging, intimacy and independence.

Butch Cassidy and the Sundance Kid (1969).
"There ain't no rules in a knife fight!"

A revival of the buddy movie (maybe it never went away). A clever script with humanly fallible characters. Two legendary outlaws at the turn of the century head out on the lam across the southwest (eventually in South America) with their female interest (Katharine Ross) in romanticized and funny robberies. However the most memorable scene occurs when Butch Cassidy and the Sundance Kid return to the hideout and find the "gang" wants to mutiny.

Cassidy suggests a duel between the hulking challenger and himself, but intimates to Sundance, "If he wins, shoot him." That exchange just sets the tone. Newman asks his opponent, "what weapons do you want to use?" They choose knives. Cassidy asks, "what are the rules?" The huge man bellows, "there's no rules in a knife fight!" and Cassidy kicks him in the crotch, bringing the fight to a swift ending. This exchange has become a classic with men across the generations.

Jimmy Stewart in *Mr. Smith Goes to Washington*, Gregory Peck in *To Kill a Mockingbird*, and Mel Gibson in *What Women Want*, have given men kinder and gentler role models.

Jack Nicholson, on the other hand, has created his own genre. In doing so he may have made things more befuddling for men.

Easy Rider. (1969) Dropping out and an unforgettable road trip.
5 Easy Pieces. (1970) A talented musician working on oilrigs and trying to make sense of his relation with his father.
Carnal Knowledge. (1971) A decadent three-decade account of Y-chromosome behavior.
One Flew Over the Cuckoo's Nest. (1975) A crazed messiah in the nut house.
The Shining. (1980) Stephen King's horror in a snowbound hotel. Jack is the main horror.

> *Terms of Endearment. (1983) A sly charming neighbor astronaut, and a tragic-comedy.*
> *A Few Good Men.* (1992) "You can't handle the truth!"
> *As Good as It Gets.* (1997) Obsessive-compulsive disorder and narcissism.

W. C. Fields (1879–1946) let us laugh at him as well as other people in his funny world. Like Woody Allen, his movies have a way of validating the saying, "Some people's role in life is to serve as a bad example." His movies included the following:

> *Pool Sharks* (1915)
> *Running Wild* (1927)
> *The Pharmacist* (1932)
> *The Dentist* (1932)
> *It's a Gift* (1934)
> *You Can't Cheat an Honest Man* (1939)
> *My Little Chicadee* (1940)
> *Never Give a Sucker an Even Break* (1941)

Women

We can assure you that two women have outdone the men in creating a resource for women's "buddy movies." The writers Peske and West (1999) wrote a marvelous and energetic book with piercing insights for the fairer sex in their book *Cinematherapy: The Girl's Guide to Movies for Every Mood.*

> You're not very bright are you? I like that in a man.
> —Marty Walker, *Body Heat*

The Girl's Guide is a resource that should never be further than an arm's length away.

Also, Mae West will be featured in a later chapter in capturing the nuances of the battle of the sexes. We don't recall Ms. West losing any battles.

Family and Generational Themes

John Cleese (of Monty Python fame) and Robin Skynner (1983) (Cleese's British psychiatrist) collaborated on an entertaining book, *Families and How to Survive Them.* The book covers a wide variety of topics including the opposite sex, unconscious attractions, parental roles, and family patterns. The Monty Python movies cited later in the book are a beacon of humor as healer. Plus the uncommon candor Cleese and Skynner generate in the book is not often available on this side of the Atlantic.

A movie that paired the Richard Burton/Elizabeth Taylor duet in an entertainingly dysfunctional marriage is a classic piece of repartee. Some dialogue from *Who's Afraid of Virginia Woolf?* (1966) captures the range of family ties that both bind and conflict. This movie (based on Edward Albee's play) debuted Mike Nichols as a director, and was awarded multiple Academy Awards in both America and Great Britain.

The middle-aged couple (George and Martha, played by Burton and Taylor) are almost permanently locked in a bitter and vicious verbal fight. On special occasions they drag their dinner guests into the fray.

Martha: Uh...you make me puke!
George: That wasn't a very nice thing to say, Martha.
Martha: That wasn't what?
George: ...a very nice thing to say.
Martha: I like your anger. I think that's what I like about you most...your anger. You're such a...such a simp! You don't even have the...the what?
George: ...guts?
Martha: Phrasemaker! Hey, put some more ice in my drink, will you?
You never put any ice in my drink. Why is that, hunh?
George: I always put ice in your drink. You eat it, that's all. It's that habit you have...chewing your ice cubes...like a cocker spaniel. You'll crack your big teeth.
Martha: They're my big teeth!
George: Some of them...some of them.
Martha: I've got more teeth than you have.
George: Two more.
Martha: Well, two more's a lot more.
George: I suppose. I suppose it's pretty remarkable considering how old you are.
Martha: You cut that out! You're not so young yourself.
George: I'm six years younger than you...I always have been and I always will be.
Martha: Well you're going bald.
George: So are you. (Pause...they both laugh) Hello, honey.
Martha: Hello. C'mon over here and give your Mommy a big sloppy kiss.
George: Oh...now...
Martha: I want a big sloppy kiss!
George: I don't want to kiss you Martha. Where are these people? Where are these people you invited over?
Martha: They stayed on to talk to Daddy...They'll be here... Why don't you want to kiss me?
George: Well, dear, if I kissed you I'd get all excited...I'd get beside myself, and I'd take you, by force, right here on the living-room rug,

and then our little guests would walk in, and...well, just think what your father would say about that?
Martha: You pig!
George: Oink, Oink!
Martha: Ha, ha, ha, HA! Make me another drink...lover.
George: My God, you can swill it down, can't you?
Martha: (Imitating a child) I'm firsty.
George: Jesus!
Martha: Look sweetheart, I can drink you under any goddamn table you want...so don't worry about me!
George: Martha, I gave you the prize years ago...there isn't an abomination award going that you...
Martha: I swear...if you existed I'd divorce you.
George: Well, just stay on your feet, that's all...These people are your guests, you know, and...
Martha: I can't even see you...I haven't been able to see for years.
George: ...I f you pass out, or throw up, or something...
Martha: ...I mean you're a blank, a cipher...
George: ...and try to keep your clothes on, too. There aren't many more sickening sights than you with a couple of drinks in you and your skirt up over your head, you know...
Martha: ... a zero...
George: ... your "heads" I should say...

> Happiness is having a large, loving, caring, close knit family in another city.
> —George Burns

"Old paint on canvas as it ages, sometimes becomes transparent. When that happens it is possible in some pictures to see the original lines; a tree will show through a women's dress, a child makes way for a dog, a larger boat is no longer on an open sea. That is called *pentimento* because the painter "repented," changed his mind. Perhaps it would be as well to say that the old conception replaced by a later choice is a way of seeing and then seeing again...The paint has aged and I want to see what was there for me once, what is there for me now.
—Lillian Hellman,
Pentimento

All sorrows can be borne if you put them in a story or tell a story about them.
—Isak Dinesen

Interlude Back to Childhood

In the area of children's movies, many Disney movies are at the same time entertaining and valuable. A quick survey of some of these (with reviews from the expert children themselves) may be an enjoyable place to start.

Toy Story, with Tom Hanks and Tim Allen, seems to be a universal favorite. Have you ever wondered what toys do when you leave the room?

This engaging tale is of the family's move and the dilemma of bringing with them all the cherished toys: Woody (the cowboy), Rex (the dinosaur), Mr. Potato Head, Slinky Dog, and dozens of others. Which will be brought to the new home and which are in danger of being discarded? Some are "mutant toys" that have been assembled from parts the boy Sid may have tossed to the floor.

At one point Sid was admonished that "from now on you must take good care of your toys. Because if you don't, we'll find out."

When the dust had settled in the new home, Woody chided Buzz Lightyear that since he had survived the cut and made it to the new home, he could relax since no toy could be worse than him.

All figured they were safe at least till Andy's next birthday. Do you think it's easy being a toy? Ask Woody and Buzz. They may not tell you to your face, but wait till you leave the room.

Other Disney movies/books with lasting meaning and effect include:

Snow White and the Seven Dwarfs
Pinocchio
Dumbo
The Jungle Book
Cinderella
Bambi
Peter Pan
Sleeping Beauty
The Rescuers Down Under
It's a Small World
The Three Little Pigs
Lady & the Tramp
Alice in Wonderland
Mother Goose
The Fox and the Hound
101 Dalmatians
The Little Mermaid
Ariel and the Secret Grotto
Winnie the Pooh and Tigger Too
Winnie the Pooh and the Blustery Day
Beauty and the Beast
Aladdin
The Lion King

Here is a little perspective from someone not of Disneyland:

> Bless the children first,
> for they need help
> just to get them safely down the block.
> With all the mazes
> that we make for them
> (like teaching them to hate before they learn to spell),
> it's a wonder that they ever find
> the door that opens out of adolescence.
>
> —author unknown, *In Order of Importance*

> Each fairy tale is a magic mirror which reflects some aspects of our inner world, and of the steps required by our evolution from immaturity to maturity. For those who immerse themselves in what the fairy tale has to communicate, it becomes a deep, quite pool which at first seems to reflect only our own image; but behind it we soon discover the inner turmoil's of our soul—its depth, and ways to gain peace within ourselves and with the world, which is the reward of our struggles.
>
> —Bruno Bettelheim, *The Uses of Enchantment*

> When we are planning for posterity, we ought to remember that virtue is not hereditary.
>
> —Thomas Paine

> In the small matters trust the mind, in the larger ones the heart.
>
> —Sigmund Freud

> Science is a first-rate piece of furniture for a man's upper chamber, if he has common sense on the ground floor.
>
> —Oliver Wendell Holmes

> There are only two or three human stories, and they go on repeating themselves as fiercely as if they had never happened before.
>
> —Willa Cather

> In every couple each person is trying to, "grow the other one up." In reality that means we want them to get better at meeting our needs.
>
> —Gus Napier, *The Family Crucible*

A remarkable book on using films to understand psychopathology is *Movies and Mental Illness: Using Film to Understand Psychopathology* (Wedding & Boyd, 1999). Their book provides countless examples of movie characters and situations, guiding us to an appreciation of diagnosis, and nudging the reader toward conceptualizing and applying an enlightened and enjoyable perspective. The book fosters therapists' ability (or anyone interested) to grasp and integrate core dynamics, accurate diagnosis, and treatment planning via the authors' well-conceived format.

A benefit in using movies to augment life experience is that we gain perspective. Things we already know and things we need to be reminded of can come together while witnessing others' dilemmas.

A lovely story is told about the young man from a farming community who has gone off to the State Agriculture College. On one of his trips home, he is talking to his dad's friend who has the homestead next to theirs. The Ag student asks the man whether he's heard about the new nitrates, which can be used to increase crop production. He also asks the older farmer whether he's considered a new crop rotation strategy which is all the rage at the A & M school. After the student mentions a few other new strategies and crop-boosting techniques that are: "hot off the presses," the neighbor tells the boy, "You know son, I don't farm half as well now as I already know how!"

This charming punch line captures a great truth. The application of knowledge is less often a matter how much we know, but rather when, where, and how to apply it.

REFERENCES

Bern, Eric (1964). *The games people play.* New York: Grove Press.
Bowen, Murray (1978). *Family therapy in clinical practice.* New York: Aronson.
Egli, D., Peake, T., Borduin, C. and Fleck, R. (1985). *Ego identity status and death perspective with older adults..* Proceedings of the American Psychological Association Convention, Los Angeles.
Erikson, Erik (1980). *Identity and the life cycle.* New York: Norton.
Erikson, Erik (1982). *The life cycle completed.* New York: Norton.
Estes Pinkola, Clarissa (1995). *Women who run with the wolves.* New York: Ballantine.
Fowler, J. W. (1981). *Stages of faith.* San Francisco: Harper & Row.
Gilligan, C., Ward, J. and Taylor (eds.) (1981). *Mapping the moral domain: A contribution of women's thinking to psychological theory and education.* Cambridge, MA: Harvard University Press.
Harris, T. H. (1973). *I'm OK—You're OK.* New York: Avon Books.
Hawley, G. A. (1988). *Measures of psychosocial development: professional manual.* Odessa, FL: Psychological Assessment Resources.
Kerr, M. and Bowen, M. (1988). *Family revaluation.* New York: Norton.
Kohlberg, Lawrence & Gilligan, Carol (1971). The adolescent as a philosopher: The discovery of the self in a postconventional world. *Daedalus, 100, 1051–1086.*
Lerner, Harriet (1985). *The dance of anger.* New York: Harper & Row.

Marcia, J. (1966). Development and validation of ego identity status. *Journal of Personality and Social Psychology, 3, 551–558.*

May, Rollo (1975). *The courage to create.* New York: Norton.

Napier, G. and Whitaker, C. (1980). *The family crucible.* New York: Bantam Books.

Peske, Nancy and West, Beverly (1999). *Cinematherapy: The girl's guide to movies for every mood.* New York: Dell.

Pipher, Mary (1994). *Reviving Ophelia: Saving the selves of adolescent girls.* New York: Grosset/Putnam

Satir, Virginia (1988). *The new people making.* Mountain View, CA: Science and Behavioral Books.

Skynner, Robin and Cleese, John (1983). *Families and how to survive them.* New York: Oxford University Press.

Titelman, P. (ed.) (1998). *Clinical applications of Bowen family systems theory.* New York: Haworth Press.

Viorst, Judith (1986). *Necessary losses.* New York: Simon & Schuster.

Wedding, D. and Boyd, M. (1999). *Movies and mental illness: Using films to understand psychopathology.* New York: McGraw Hill College.

White, M. and Epston, D. (1990). *Narrative means to therapeutic ends.* New York: Norton.

2
The Power and Possibilities of Cinema

We all try to make sense of ourselves and our world. Some of us do it in earnest. Some do it defensively. Some of us pursue it with irony. We value and savor cherished experiences. Some may wish to divert their gaze from experiences that overwhelmed, and some may wish to manage with mirth. A story brings meaning together in a form or theme. We very much live our lives in terms of stories and themes. Some are personal accounts and some are shared by families, friends, and cultures or kindred communities. In research, shared communities or groups are called *cohorts*. To me that sounds like some kind of a fish. Please accept my apologies for whenever I have to use the word *cohort*. Try not to think about fish. Or go ahead if you want to.

In our culture cinema and other visual media are everywhere. Friends and parents teach children and young adults to enjoy and value books and classic literature. These teachers require and recommend classic written wisdom to young and old minds. Sometimes books are less popular and in some ways less dramatic to the generations weaned on television, cinema, and now cyberspace. When training health professionals, we want to help them recognize, understand, and act effectively in caring for people. Movies are a great medium to help challenge people, change them and help them grow. Those we help may need to laugh, mourn, or strengthen their resolve. Movies and their rich legacy (often rooted in good literature) heighten emotional as well as logical growth. And film can help us rethink the ways we relate to our world.

Stories help us live our lives and may help others live theirs. First, narratives help us develop and maintain a sense of self. They also help us recognize resources and shared themes. Second, stories give choices on how to live our lives. Swapping stories affords comparison shopping. Third, narratives give order to the sometimes chaotic events of our lives. The quote, "Life is what happens to us when we're planning something else," captures that meaning in a dramatic fashion. Cinema offers a wide, rich, funny, frightening, redeeming and ironic array of possibilities and stories. Movies also have a habit of slipping past our "mind's logic police" and immersing us in the recognition drama. A fourth value is that we can also listen to our own stories. The narrator's role is an active agent persuading and drawing on stories and experiences, some that worked or some that flopped. Our cultures are guided by stories or points of view, some more popular than others. And finally, the most compelling argument for the value of cinema is how much more you would be affected by what we are saying if it were well-presented in a powerful film.

We need to sample others' stories and to have our own stories told and heard. Sometimes we give good advice but do a poor job of following it. In life at the times we need to be the most creative, we are often the least creative because we are stressed or demoralized. The pressure to make sense of things is clouded by fear, panic, or poor models. Therapists have their own stories about themselves but also about how therapy works (Viney, 1993). That discernment is an exciting force, and if we can make it enjoyable, so much the better.

WHAT THIS BOOK IS, AND WHAT IT IS NOT

This is not a traditional guide book on how to do psychotherapy. It is not a psychotherapy cookbook. It is less about precision diagnosis and matching technique to a particular client. Rather it is more about recognizing universal conundrums, tragedies, and triumphs that people meet in their unfolding lives. The book is not a catalog of empirically supported therapy techniques, but a map of persistent problems and time-honored answers to life challenges. Core themes that evolve across the life span can be understood through good literature or cinema. There is an advantage of distance and perspective when we can read about or watch and feel for someone else's life puzzles. That vantage point gives us room to cry, laugh, ponder, and consider the options. These themes, tragedies, or opportunities can become understandable scripts with a range of solutions. The film medium provides a vivification of these puzzles, pains, and possibilities. Sometimes in psychology we call these core dynamics. The core patterns are nestled in life stages and life challenges.

> There are three rules for writing a novel. Unfortunately, no one knows what they are.
> —W. Somerset Maugham

This funny quote by Maugham aside, it is possible to highlight a wide variety of life challenges ("dynamics" in psychology parlance) from which we can predict, recognize, learn, and solve. Each solution gained, gives new resources and possibilities for the future. These conundrums are predictable passages addressed in a little more detail under the Erikson scheme of life stages in Chapter 4.

PRACTICING DISCERNMENT

Hopefully the book is an entertaining way to learn, grow, and apply emotional learning. It offers a way to practice emotional and interpersonal learning through the drama of cinema as we better grasp core dynamics or themes. The other important value is that it recognizes prevalent problems, it can apply the "minimal interference principle." This strategy is simply that we don't make any more change than necessary when helping others through difficult times. It has been suggested that there is a finite number of "core dynamics" that plague humanity. This book won't answer that question with certainty now, but it is a good premise. When a pattern is clear from the vantage of some emotional distance, we can be creative in our solution. Cinema gives us an endless source of emotional and interpersonal puzzles and solutions.

Mining these stories can be redeeming, enlightening or just plain entertaining. From immersion to a strategy of escape, the view of someone else's life always offers new possibilities.

MOVIES THAT PROVOKE, ENLIGHTEN, CLARIFY, OBFUSCATE, INSPIRE, AND ENTERTAIN

The good, the bad, (the ugly) and the popular is another way to classify movies. It is said that art imitates life. Life also imitates art. Consider a classic funny example.

Being There (1979)

Peter Sellers, Melvyn Douglas, Shirley MacLaine. A memorably odd film about a feeble-minded gardener (Chauncey Gardener) whose entire knowledge of life comes from watching television. (It seems reasonable to stretch the analogy to movie junkies). Jerszy Kosinski adapted the film from his novel. When his employer dies, Sellers is thrust into the strange role of a mysterious sage. With his prized remote control unit, and the odd circumstances, he is thrust into politics and welcomed as a wise advisor, soothsayer or pundit.

One of the funniest lines in the movie was Chauncey's unintentional double entendre: "I like to watch." The person listening to him thinks Chauncey meant watching the sex scene on the screen, rather than his simple-minded fascination with *anything* on TV.

Sellers' other contributions, such as *The Magic Christian* (1969), *A Shot in the Dark*, *Dr. Strangelove* (both 1964), *The Mouse That Roared* (1959), and *The World of Henry Orient* (1964) left a unique film influence. Through his offbeat humor he mocked our funny pretensions.

As mentioned in the first chapter, there are predictable changes in individuals and relationships. Growth often evolves through alternating or competing processes. The processes are markers to help chart growth or help people grow when they get stuck. Movies may give us perspective to see whether the person needs stabilization or change? Recall Jack (the dermatologist turned psychiatrist quoted in the introduction) who planned the scope of treatment by whether a problem needed opened or closed to heal.

Movies' range of benefits include:

> hopes, fears and fascinations,
> cultural conscience and enlightenment,
> fashion and substance,
> enchantment and captivation, and
> pure entertainment or escape.

Mining for Stories

Erving Polster (1987) was a Gestalt psychotherapist who suggested that stories provide multiple benefits for therapy, entertainment and fascination. These include escape from the present (or escape into another's present, past or future) a fascination which bypasses logic, spotlighting or elaborating meaning, rhythms, and entrancement, plus a way to translate complexity into coherence.

Psychology has borrowed the German concept of *Zeitgeist* (translated as spirit of the times) to explain social factors that affect psychology and vice versa. Movies are entertaining archives to understand eras, shared history or period pieces. Movies, along with books, music and poetry, may rewrite history in ways that clarify, elaborate or even revise the facts.

> What logic can't grasp metaphor can. Metaphor is the hand thrust under the water catching live fish. Metaphor is a passageway between fantasy and logic; it will take you someplace new.
>
> In response to the question why Southerners are such good storytellers...The civil war had its contribution.
> It is said about wars...
> The winners write history and the losers write poetry.
> Irony is the ability to look at yourself clearly and still get the joke.
> —Blanch McCrary Boyd, *The Red Neck Way of Knowledge*

In London there is a time-honored tradition of poets being showcased on the *Underground* (their subway). Historically the *Underground* was a place that saved the lives of many during the bombing in World War II. A long legacy of art, music, cinema, and verse captures certain eras, as well as emotions that endure. Poetry and other art may save people's spirit in times of peace as well as in times of war.

> A thing of beauty is a joy forever:
> Its loveliness increases; it will never
> Pass into nothingness; but still will keep
> A bower quiet for us, and a sleep
>
> Full of sweet dreams, and health, and quiet breathing.
> —John Keats, "A Thing of Beauty" (p. 53), *Poems on the Underground* (Cassell Publishers, 1995)

In my craft or sullen art
Exercised in the still night
When only the moon rages
And the lovers lie abed
With all their grief's in their arm.
I labor by singing light
Not for ambition or bread
Or the strut and trade of charms
On the ivory stages
But for the common wages
of their most secret heart.

—Dylan Thomas, "In My Craft or Sullen Art" (p. 72), *Poems on the Underground (*New Directions Publishers, 1946)

Cinema can be both above ground and underground. It can also earn more than just "common" wages.

Classic silent films should also be mentioned. Charlie Chaplin is the reigning king of that genre. Perhaps silent movies could be a sequel to this book.

Movies provide multiple sensory channels. This venue draws on the same sources that psychotherapy will do well to study. Visual, tactile (think about the seats and maybe the gum on the seat in front of you), and auditory dimensions are all used. Movies are right-brain, left-brain, and all the layers and connections in between. To borrow the wisdom of a favorite professor, as therapists we need to appeal to the mind's logic but also reach the "lizard brain." This primitive part of the mind includes the visceral or gut reactions triggered in times of stress, fear, and lust. The more senses involved, the more lasting the impact. Movies and theater confront, smuggle, provoke, and send a vast array of messages.

Both subtle and direct influences reside in the music of movies. Profound meanings in songs and musical scores permeate and amplify the lasting effect and emotional fervor. Movie award galas like the Academy Awards, Cannes Film Festival, Sundance Awards and so on, realize and honor this powerful dimension. The emotional effect of songs and musical scores make the experience last long beyond logic.

The sensory channels have friends in psychology. The work of noted hypnotherapists such as Erika Fromm (1976, 1981) or Milton Erickson (1954) convey an appreciation of levels and channels of consciousness as well as strategies to understand, influence, and improve the quality of life. A school of influence called *neurolinguistic programming* (don't be too put-off by the ominous name) offers an intriguing explanation of the interaction between sensory modalities (visual, tactile, auditory; right brain, left brain) and emotional understanding. Using these principles and channels can both entertain and promote growth, healing and change (Bandler & Grinder, 1975, 1976).

People have subtle preferences in the way that they perceive and respond to sensory information. For instance, the authors Bandler and Grinder studied the style, technique and strategies of "master therapists" (such as Virginia Satir, Milton Erickson, Fritz Perls, and others) to determine what makes them so effective. They also looked at the characteristics of people effective in sales and persuasion jobs to determine what makes them effective in "closing a deal" or selling ideas. The findings showed that people have preferred sensory channels (sight, sound, touch, taste, and smell). And the best communicator/persuaders know how to subtly "join" people and use these sensory portals to influence them. The persuasion does not have to lead to a "sale," but just as importantly the selected strategies can amplify a message, meaning or preferred course of action. Preferred representational systems are secret passageways to seeing, feeling, believing, and persuading.

Over the years movies have used the full range of sensory influence, from the visual and auditory to tactual and gustatory (e.g., 3-D glasses, wiring seats in horror movies, introducing smells and selling lots of popcorn and other snacks). Music stands out as a powerful amplifier, mood guider, and emotional enhancer. Academy Awards for music score as well as visual effects are crucial. We are not aware of awards for concession-stand quality, but that dimension has its place. There are even movies about cannibals, but that is an acquired taste.

Music helps make cinema memorable, in ways both subtle and profound. In the same way therapists can be more effective when messages permeate emotionally through multiple sensory modalities. The messages last longer when memories or feelings are amplified through all the heart's and mind's portals. It may be that the more senses involved, the more lasting the effect.

Jung (1964) said that the members of our society who convey the lover archetype are painters, poets, musicians, composers, and sculptors. He did not mention film makers, but film was in its infancy in his lifetime. A multitude of creative voices and visions must come together in cinema. And there is no guarantee that one creative medium translates easily to another. Jung's approach to dream analysis provides a structure that can enhance and sharpen therapists' ability to understand themes, hopes, and dreams. Jung suggested that in dreams, all the topics, characters and emotions are viable dimensions. Conscious, uncconscious and what he called the collective unconscious are possible paths to uderstanding. Cinema provides another window to our motives, helps and hindrances to happy lives.

Rollo May's view of creativity as a balance of form and passion, has already been mentioned, and will be a recurrent theme in this book. Balancing form and passion is a core process of human growth, as well as a defining process in art and literature. An additional benefit to understanding creative processes is that the same skills allow therapists and their clients to understand the motives, hopes, fears, and solutions that lead to personal and emotional growth and resilience. Movies can be a venue to conceptualize hopes, fears, problems, and human solutions. These multichannel lessons can both entertain and help people. Or as the Roman satirist Horace said, "It can both teach and delight!"

APPENDIX

Included as an appendix to this chapter is the format/syllabus for a course on aging. An outline and a short bibliograpy and list of movies are incorporated to suggest ways to use cinema in training practicioners. Chapter 7 also addresses issues in life stages and conceptualization.

Movie Options for a Course on Aging

The following list of movies has been a valuable adjunct to our doctoral clinical course on aging and adult development. Students like the format and can extract great material to practice case conceptualization and treatment planning. One focus in the course is on problems of aging and understanding medical, psychological and existential complications which may arise with individuals and families. A unifying theme in the course is two-fold, based on the book, *Healthy Aging, Healthy Treatment: The Impact of Telling Stories*, (Praeger, 1998).

The *first theme* is that aging well includes psychological, physical, and spiritual dimensions. However, the cultures of medicine, religion, and psychology often "do not play well together" in advancing optimal growth in the later years. An article by Estes and Binney (1989), "The Biomedicalization of Aging," describes our overblown belief that medicine and technology will protect us from our fears of growing old. Health care includes three parts: (1) prevention, (2) diagnosis/treatment and (3) rehabilitation. The majority of our country's health care resources are spent on advancing the second part: *technology* in diagnosis and acute treatment. Prevention and rehabilitation are under-funded in an era of managed care. Health professionals may be among the most ageist group (along with seniors themselves) in the United States and Great Britain. One of Dr. Seuss's last books, *You're Only Old Once*, is a funny and telling account of what health care inadvertently does to confound the search for good health care. I often give copies of the book to senior patients who laugh at the familiar aggravations or to health care colleagues who need to be jolted.

The *second theme* is that identity for individuals and families is a life story. Who we are may be thought of as life story construction. Psychological or physical illnesses are examples of a life story gone awry and psychotherapy or other forms of healing may be thought of as story repair. Among these writers are: Gutmann (1987), Howard (1991), Kaufman (1986), Chinen (1989), Peake (1998), Omer (1993), Birren and Deutchman (1991), Josselson (1978 and 1996), Viney (1993), Viorst (1986), O'Hanlon Hudson and Hudson O'Hanlon (1991) and Friedan (1993), to name a few. Often life is what happens to us when we're planning something else. The "minimal interference principle" is the therapy notion that we make no more changes than necessary. We should preserve what worked for people in the past and change the things that don't. We all encounter necessary losses. Life stories and stages can be written, reconsidered, revised and renewed to reinvent ourselves and our families.

The movies marked with an asterisk have proven especially valuable in discussions of how families, cultures and life stages may help or hinder "a good old age." They also show ways to help seniors and their families reconsider, reshape and rewrite their life stories, saving the best and rewriting the phases (or chapters) that challenge. I would welcome your comments or additions for cinema as a painless provocative, entertaining and renewing vehicle for training ourselves our students and learning from older adults.

Movies

*1. *The Trip to Bountiful* (Geraldine Page, Rebecca De Mornay)
*2. *The Last of His Tribe* (John Voigt, Graham Greene)
*3. *Fried Green Tomatoes* (Kathy Bates, Jessica Tandy, Mary Stuart Masterson)
*4. *Used People* (Shirley MacLaine, Marcello Mastroianni, Jessica Tandy)
5. *On Golden Pond* (Katharine Hepburn, Henry Fonda, Jane Fonda)
6. *Grumpy Old Men* (Walter Mathau, Jack Lemmon, Ann Margaret)
*7. *Nobody's Fool* (Paul Newman, Jessica Tandy)
8. *Cocoon* (Jessica Tandy, Hume Cronyn, Steve Guttenberg, Wilford Brimley)
*9. *A Walk in the Clouds* (Anthony Quinn, Keanu Reeves, Aitana Sanchez-Gijon)
*10. *Wrestling Ernest Hemingway* (Robert Duvall, Richard Harris, Piper Laurie)
*11. *To Dance with the White Dog* (Jessica Tandy, Hume Cronyn)
12. *Driving Miss Daisy* (Jessica Tandy, Morgan Freeman)
13. *The Shadow Box* (Joanne Woodward, Christopher Plummer, Valerie Harper)
*14. *A Gathering of Old Men* (Louis Gossett, Richard Widmark, Holly Hunter)
15. *Nothing in Common* (Tom Hanks, Jackie Gleason)
16. *Steel Magnolias* (Shirley MacLaine, Olympia Dukakis, Sally Field, Dolly Parton)
17. *Parenthood* (Steve Martin, Mary Steenburgen Jason Robards, Keanu Reeves)
18. *Twilight Zone Montage* (excerpt on retirement home)

REFERENCES

Bandler, R. and Grinder, J. (1975). *Patterns of the hypnotic techniques of Milton Erickson, M.D. Volumes I & II.* Cupertino, CA: Meta Publications.

Bandler, R. and Grinder, J. (1976) *The structure of magic: I & II: A book about language and therapy (I):* and *A book about communication and change.* Palo Alto, CA: Science and Behavior Books.

Benson, G. Chernaik, J. and Herbert, C. (eds. (1995). *Poems on the underground,* 5th ed. London: Cassell Publishers.

Birren, J. and Deutchman, D. (1991). *Guiding autobiography groups for older adults.* Baltimore: Johns Hopkins University Press

Boyd, Blanche McCrary (1971, 1995). *The red neck way of knowledge.* New York: Vintage.

Chinen, A. (1989). *In the everafter: Fairy tales for the second half of life.* Wilmette, IL: Chiron Publishers.

Erikson, Milton (1954). Special techniques of brief hypnotherapy. *Journal of Clinical and Experimental Hypnosis, 2,* 109–129.

Estes, C. and Binney, E. (1989). The biomedicalization of aging: Dangers and dilemmas. *The Gerontologist, 29,* 587–596.

Friedan, Betty. (1993). *The fountain of age.* New York: Simon & Schuster.

Fromm, Erika (1976). Altered states of consciousness and ego psychology. *Social Science Review, 50,* 557–569.

Fromm, Erika (1981). Primary and secondary process in waking and in altered states of consciousness. *Academic Psychology Bulletin, 3,* 29–45.

Gordon, David (1978). *Therapeutic metaphors: Helping others through the looking glass.* Cupertino, CA: Meta Publications.

Gutmann, D. (1987). *Reclaimed powers: Toward a new psychology of men and women in later life.* New York: Basic Books.

Howard, G. (1991). Culture tales: A narrative approach to thinking, cross-cultural psychology, and psychotherapy. *American Psychologist, 46,* 187–197.

Josselson, R. (1978). *Finding herself: Pathways to identity development in women.* San Francisco: Jossey-Bass.

Josselson, R. (1996). *Revising herself: The story of women's identity.* Oxford: Oxford University Press.

Jung, C. (1964). *Man and his symbols.* Garden City, New York: Doubleday.

Kaufman, S. (1986). *The ageless self: Sources of meaning in late life.* New York: Meridian.

May, Rollo (1975). *The courage to create.* New York: Norton.

O'Hanlon Hudson, P. & Hudson O'Hanlon, W. (1991). *Rewriting love stories: Brief marital therapy.* New York: Norton.

Omer, H. (1993). Short-term psyotherapy and the rise of the life sketch. Psychotherapy, 30, 668–673

Peake, T. (1998). *Healthy aging, healthy treatment: The impact of telling stories.* Westport, CT: Praeger.

Pitman, Frank, M.D. *The screening room,* an ongoing column for *The Family Therapy Networker.*

Polster, Erving (1987). *Every person's life is worth a novel.* New York: Norton.

Seuss, Dr. (1986). *You're only old once!* New York: Random House.

Viney, L. (1993). *Life stories: Personal construct therapy with the elderly.* New York: Wiley.

Viorst, J. (1986). *Necessary losses.* New York: Wiley.

Vogler, C. V. (1998). *The writer's journey: Mythic structure for writers.* Studio City, CA: M. Wise Productions.

3
Medical, Spiritual, and Psychological Dimensions

Growth, health, and healing have physical, psychological, and spiritual dimensions. T he body, mind, and spirit may have their cultures in our society. How are these cultures or world views portrayed in movies and life? When and how do they help and when do they hinder? Consider a few examples as they appear in movies and see what insights and themes emerge.

In a previous book I suggested that a life-long process of growth, healing, and maturation involves medical, spiritual and psychological dimensions (Peake, 1998). However, the purveyors of these belief systems each has its own "culture." Viktor Frankl, a famous psychiatrist and survivor of German concentration camps, stressed that an appreciation of the spiritual dimension must be considered in diagnosing and treating problems of soma and psyche (*The Doctor & the Soul*, 1973). For that reason the portrayal of these dimensions in movies, and in training health professionals, can be a gold mine of vivid problems that occur when one dimension is overvalued or ignored. On the other hand, the benefits of honoring all three facets are compelling. Wise stories can light the path of life's twists and turns. Watching, listening, and considering others stories thoughtfully benefits the teller and the audience. A wise friend once said that some people's role in life is to serve as a bad example. Movies have plenty of those. Life's seasons and story lines appear differently from the vantage of different ages, stages, and cultures.

Storytelling and story-tending create a rich tapestry that can honor, intrigue, shame, enlighten, humor, entertain and renew our personal "hunches" about life's journey. The three cultures of growth, healing, and renewal can be dramatized through movies, and increase our understanding. With all three dimensions included, the impact is more enduring. Humor also goes a long way to smuggle new understandings. So, the adage that "some things are too important to be taken seriously," mixes well with movies and the culture of healing.

The medical, spiritual, and psychological cultures of perspectives are previewed in order to consider understanding their contributions to health and healing:

Medical (disease vis-a-vis illness). An important distinction in health care is the difference between disease and illness. The concept of disease may be the doctor's vantage, while illness incorporates the personal and subjective experience of the sufferer. As we consider this important distinction, there are many movies from which to draw. The focus may be on the culture of hospitals; the angst, arrogance, or humanity of physicians. The culture of medicine has spawned a number of anthropological explorations of hospitals as their own society. There are many movies that show the personal side of joy and despair. Since health, growth, sickness and healing are a large part of life development; this medical domain provides a lot of models in cinema.

Spiritual (psychology of Religion). Wulff (1991) did an admirable job in describing the psychology of religion from an academic perspective. We know that psychology and medicine have great value, but also very real limitations. Movies have painted both good and bad pictures of religion and spirituality, not unlike real life. In this chapter we want to sample some movies that enlighten. We will look at some of the ideas of Paul Tillich and Rollo May. Good movies have been used to convey notions such as love, forgiveness, healing, salvation, sins of omission or commission, grace, and unconditional love.

Zeitgeist is a German word that means *spirit of the times*. This concept considers ideas, styles, or movements that are in vogue or have their own place under the sun. Conversely, a concept of *times of the spirit* is a useful notion to explore in cinema. The spiritual realm is an important dimension to include when healing lives and training therapists.

Psychological. Applications of psychology in movies are well represented. Later we will consider a number of good and bad examples about therapy. There are an array of films that portray both how to, and how not to, practice the care of the psyche. Our experience has been that sampling these movie examples always stirs discussion and thoughtful application.

Cinema examples from each of these three perspectives (or dimensions) offer ways to understand people's hunches, convictions, and motivations as portrayed in films.

MEDICAL

Consider a few movie examples.

The Hospital (1971). G. C. Scott. Something of a cult favorite, this is a savage, sarcastic, unrelenting look at a chaotic metropolitan hospital. Everything from ineptitude, mid-life crises, witchdoctors, and murder combine

Medical, Spiritual, and Psychological Dimensions 45

to portray the hospital as a strange culture. Diana Rigg, Stockard Channing, and Bernard Hughes keep the mix a constant bubbling cauldron. Written by Paddy Chayevsky and directed by Arthur Hiller, the film won the Academy Award (both American and British) for best screenplay, and Scott was nominated for best actor. Great cinema to get discussions flowing.

Article 99 (1992). Doctors in a Kansas City Veteran's Administration Hospital try to heal patients while putting up with bureaucratic red tape and a stingy administrator. When the rogue physician (Ray Liotta) is dismissed the patients hold a siege.

Patch Adams (1998). Robin Williams stars in this story of an unusual medical student who had some problems of his own earlier in life. Hunter "Patch" Adams takes to treating terminally patients with compassion, laughter, and other unorthodox techniques. Based on a true story, the movie is a good one to prompt discussion on the soul as well as the science of healing.

The Doctor (1991). William Hurt. An excellent portrayal of the physician having to come to grips with the personal experience of illness. It is based on the book, *A Taste of My Own Medicine*, by Dr. Edward Rosenbaum. Hurt's character learns respect and compassion, which were previously absent from his own repertoire. This movie has been effectively used in medical ethics courses to stir up discussion.

Awakenings (1990). Robert De Niro and Robin Williams star in this true story based on Oliver Sacks's book of the same title. Sacks, a famous neurologist, experimented with using L-Dopa (Levodopa), which is effective in treating Parkinson's disease. Sacks tried it with catatonic patients who had been "sleeping' for as long as 30 years. Music by Randy Newman reverberates well throughout this touching and tragic tale. The movie was nominated for Academy Awards in categories of best screenplay, best picture and best actor (De Niro).

The Citadel (1938). Robert Donat, Rosalind Russell, Rex Harrison. Based on the A. J. Cronin novel, an honest and intelligent drama about a young British doctor who is morally corrupted by as he moves to a lucrative practice city practice, from his poor home mining village. He treats wealthy hypochondriacs. The film was also nominated for several Academy Awards.

*M*A*S*H* (1970). One of Robert Altman's directing masterpieces, which is judged by the American Film Institute as one of the top 100 movies of all time. A monumental irrevernt, hilarious, and well-cast black comedy about a group of surgeons and nurses at a mobile army surgical hospital in Korea. Many people are more familiar with the long-running TV series, which was based on the film. The combination of notable cast (Donald Sutherland, Elliot Gould, Tom Skerritt, Sally Kellerman, Jo Ann Pflug, Gary Burghoff, Robert Duvall) and the risky genre (at the time) captured the country's frustration with Vietnam (once removed by a decade more or less). This film also set the tone for

Altman's trademark efforts and probably influenced national opinion that brought the war to a close.

The Elephant Man (1980). This is the biography of John Merrick, a severely deformed man, who with the help of his sympathetic doctor moved from freak shows into London's society. Anthony Hopkins, Anne Bancroft, John Hurt. This was the first mainstream film for director David Lynch.

Carlson and Shield (1989) have written an excellent book called *Healers on Healing,* which looks at the experience of physicians from the personal and subjective perspective on how the profession affects them and the people they treat.

SPIRITUAL: EXISTENTIAL/RELIGIOUS

> A clear conscience is often the sign of a bad memory.
> —Anonymous

> A difference of opinion is what makes horse racing and missionaries.
> —Will Rogers

The theologian Paul Tillich has had wide influence in spiritual, philosophical and psychological circles. Rollo May's ideas and writing were influenced by Tillich's mentoring. Carl Roger's contributions in *Client-Centered Therapy* (1965) lean heavily on the concept of "unconditional positive regard." This special interpersonal acceptance increases the value of technique in treatment. Martin Buber (1958) also insists that a healing relationship is fostered by the acceptance that comes from the special personal "I and Thou," accepting quality. The psychiatrist Viktor Frankl (1997) has made important contributions to integrating psychological, medical, and spiritual dimensions. The varied contributions are compelling and hope-engendering.

Many movies are available to entertain and clarify spiritual themes. Some of these pictures may be worth a thousand words. The clergy, Charles Cooper *(cooper@hotmail.com)* has been kind enough to lend some of his thoughts on current movies and Tillich's themes of puzzlement, shortcomings, despair, grace, and renewal. A web site on religious themes is included with other references at the conclusion of the chapter.

Amistad (1997). Steven Spielberg again creates an epic from another historic example of man's inhumanity to man. Based on a true story, it is the saga of fifty-three African slaves who escape from their shackles on a stormy night off the coast of Cuba. They attempt to sail back to Africa but are tricked by Spanish navigators and end up off the coast of Connecticut. Arrested by U.S. officials, they are charged with murder and piracy. John Quincy Adams (Anthony Hopkins) comes out of retirement to plead their cause before the Supreme Court. The prisoners show inspiring dignity and determination, surpassing their captor persecutors.

Medical, Spiritual, and Psychological Dimensions   47

Theme: Principalities and Powers (the New Being)

Shadowlands (1993). Director Richard Attenborough picked an unlikely couple to be the focus: Debra Winger (*Terms of Endearment; An Officer and a Gentleman*) and Anthony Hopkins (*Silence of the Lambs, Legends of the Fall, Nixon*). Hopkins portrays C.S. Lewis, the popular Oxford professor who was famous for his science fiction, children's, his literary criticism, and palatable theology.

Winger is an American divorcee who admires his work. Their courtship and eventual marriage follow a slow and winding path of the clergy's cluelessness about sex and clumsiness in experiencing the deep and abiding love about which he writes. Her belief is that making another person happier is one of life's purposes on earth. Her terminal illness challenges him to truly face his beliefs.

A funny interchange with her teaching him about sex goes like this:

Her: "What do you do when you go to bed?"
Him: "I put on my pajamas and say my prayers and get under the covers."
Her: "Well, then that's what I want you to do right now, except that when you get under the covers, I'll be there."

Theme: Love Is Stronger Than Death (the New Being)

Tender Mercies (1983). Mack Sledge (Robert Duvall) is a country and western singer past his performing prime. But he is advanced in his personal self-fulfilling prophecies about the drinkin', cheatin', and self-destructin' honky-tonk life. Rosalee (Tess Harper) is the widowed owner of a motel where he crashes, hitting bottom. Duvall offers to work off the money he owes and stays on. He finds redemption and love with Harper, marrying her and helping raise her son. A journalist hunts him down to inform him that his ex-wife is getting rich off songs he wrote. Duvall performed all the music in the film and also wrote some of the songs.

His adult daughter (Ellen Barkin) comes to visit him and reconnect, but she is later killed in a car wreck. In a key scene he says, "I never did trust happiness." However, he does create relationships that endure. The concept of "grace, " or unconditional regard (important in psychology and spirituality)
gets vivid treatment.

Theme: You Are Accepted (the Shaking of the Foundations)

Dead Man Walking (1995). Sean Penn, Susan Sarandon. Based on the fictional book by Sister Helen Prejean. Penn's character is a convicted murderer and rapist who is sentenced to execution. The nun spritual advisor (Sarandon) finds him an arrogant trash-talking racist. Sister Prejean is challenged by others and herself on how she can lend comfort to someone like him. She is also exposed to everyone else's pain. This film is an example of faith with no easy answers.

48   Cinema and Life Development

Theme: To Whom Much Is Forgiven (the New Being)

Phenomenon (1996). John Travolta, Kyra Sedgwick, Forest Whitaker, Robert Duvall. A true allegory. George (Travolta) is knocked to the ground by a brilliant light from the night sky and begins to experience startling powers of concentration, speed reading, and matchmaking. Arguments erupt with the townspeople and neighbors about his powers and motives. His own caring and sensibilities, not his special powers, make him a true phenomenon. Themes: On the transitories of life, and the depth of existence [the shaking of the foundations, and the new being]). Travolta has a knack for these spiritual interpretations when you add the other angel movie *Michael* (1996), which actually gives him atypical archangel status with a *joi de vivre* rarely equaled. Do not miss this film for entertainment and an unforgettable "road trip," movie.

Babette's Feast (1989). Adapted from Isak Dinesen by the director, Gabriel Axel. In Danish with English subtitles. The story of a culinary genius who spends fourteen years in Jutland preparing prosaic fish stew (excuse the mixed metaphor) for the local townspeople, until she suddenly comes into an unexpected fortune. She surprises the lackluster natives by preparing a monumental feast in her former French culinary style. Issues include a story of waste, a quiet debate on the right to hoard one's talents, to give them freely or simply to sell them. Babette's beautiful face, her singing voice like a rich sauce, and her healthy stride are set against the primness of religious sisters who had taken her in.

During a remarkable dinner, Babette transforms the stern puritans by the cuisine, the champagne, and the spirit of the evening. Eccentricities abound, but Babbette creates an elusive true faith, life, and fellowship.

Themes: Holy Waste and the Meaning of Joy (the New Being)

The Green Mile (1999).   Tom Hanks, Michael Clarke Duncan (Academy Award), Bonnie Hunt, Graham Greene. A spiritual allegory. The director Frank Darabont adapts a second Stephen King prison drama (the first was *The Shawshank Redemption*). Set in a cell block in 1935, Hank's character as an old man in a nursing home reveals his flashback to the strange experiences of that earlier time. Hanks presided over the execution wing of cell block E. One of the inmates is the huge, gentle, and spiritual black man (John Coffey, played by Duncan) is even afraid of the dark, but possesses strange healing powers.

Wild Bill Wharton is the archetypal evil murderer, and a prison guard also does a good job of doubling the amount of evil on the cell block. The story unfolds with a mix of power and humanity that lingers.

Themes: Healing (the New Being) Heal the Sick, Cast Out Demons (the Eternal Now)

American Beauty (1999). Kevin Spacey, Annette Bening, Thora Birch. Best Picture Academy Award (1999). A story of midlife awakening and a teasing fatalism. Social satire, tragedy, youth versus later life themes, and hypocrisy lay a troubling array of questions. The movie paints a powerful visual contrast via the family's home with beige interiors punctuated by vivid bursts of crimson red—the colors of blood and roses.

Theme: The Good That I Will Do Not (the Eternal Now)

To Kill a Mockingbird (1962). Multiple Academy Award wins and nominations. Best actor (Gregory Peck), best adapted screenplay (Horton Foote), best art/set direction, best picture, best director, best supporting actress, best score (Elmer Bernstein). Ranked 34 on the American Film Institute's 100 Greatest American Films.

This is one of the finest family-oriented movies ever made. Atticus Finch (Peck) as the small town Alabama lawyer chooses to defend a black man wrongfully accused of rape and assault on a young white woman. The genius of the production is in its success in telling the story at both the level of children and the very real and frightening adult level of hatred and cultural bigotry. Boo Radley (Robert Duvall) is brilliant in conveying so much nonverbally about the power of evil and redemption. A treasure of moral instruction.

To Kill a Mockingbird is revisited in Chapter 5 under issues of race and culture. The messages of the film warrant consideration from many perspectives.

Themes: Doing the Truth (the Shaking of the Foundations)
What Is Truth? (the New Being)

> Grace strikes us when we are in great pain and restlessness. It strikes us when our disgust for our own being, our weakness, our hostility, and our lack of direction and composure have become intolerable to us. It strikes us when, year after year, the longed-for perfection of life does not appear, when the old compulsions reign with us as they have for decades. Sometime at that moment a wave of light breaks into our darkness, and it is as though a voice were saying: "You are accepted..."
>
> —Paul Tillich, *The Shaking of the Foundations*

> I consider myself a Hindu, Christian, Moslem, Jew, Buddhist, and Confucian.
>
> —Ghandi

Elie Wiesel's book *Night* (1982) is a terrifying account of the Nazi death camp. Several movies have addressed this holocaust with different treatments.

Schindler's List (1993). Liam Neeson, Ben Kingsley.
Jakob the Liar (1999). Robin Williams, Alan Arkin, Hannah Taylor Gordon.

Life Is Beautiful (1998). Roberto Benigni (Academy Award, Best Actor).

The enduring themes in these movies convey compassion, humor, hope, and eternal values that triumph even in the face of death and evil.

And several other films convey a mystical dimension to foster growth and change.

Chocolat (2001). A French village in 1959 wrestles with morality, spirituality, and passion (in the form of chocolate).
E.T. (1982). Drew Barrymore.
Places in the Heart (1984). Sally Field, John Malkovich, Danny Glover.
The Apostle (1997). Robert Duvall, Miranda Richardson, Farrah Fawcett.

Rheinhold Niebuhr is important to mention as someone who integrated spirituality with medicince and psychology. Most people are familiar with the serenity prayer that is at the heart of Alcoholics Anonymous (and other twelve-step programs). Niebuhr was an American religious and social leader (1892–1971). He graduated from Yale Divinity School and taught at the Union Theological Seminary. The prayer was adapted from his work:

God grant me Serenity to accept the things I cannot change,

Courage to change the things I can,

and the Wisdom to know the difference.

This meditation captures an integration of the "three cultures" of medicine, psychology, and spirituality, with an enduring focus and inspiration.

Nothing worth doing is completed in our lifetime;
Therefore, we are saved by hope.
Nothing true or beautiful or good makes complete sense in any immediate context of history;
Therefore, we are saved by faith.
Nothing we do, however virtuous, can be accomplished alone;
Therefore, we are saved by love.
No virtuous act is quite as virtuous from the standpoint of our friend or foe
as from our own
Therefore, we are saved by the final form of love which is forgiveness.
—Reinhold Niebuhr, *We Must Be Saved*

PSYCHOLOGICAL: MUTATIVE METAPHORS IN PSYCHOTHERAPY

This section about therapy and its vicissitude is intentionally more of a preview than a comprehensive treatment.

Irving Yalom's (1989) book on therapy, *Love's Executioner and Other Tales of Psychotherapy*, is a valuable collection of therapy from a gifted therapist and writer whose expertise has crafted therapy with individuals, groups and medical and existential perspectives.

Arnold Lazuras' (1997) book, *Brief but Comprehensive Psychotherapy: The Multimodel Way*.is an excellent integrative format that takes into account psychological, interpersonal, and biological considerations.

Jerome and Julia Frank's (1991) book, *Persuasion and Healing* has been updated three times and continues to be the quintessential volume on the qualities that are common to all forms of effective psychotherapy.

Jerome Frank helps us understand that (besides their symptoms) therapy patients are demoralized. Something has left them feeling ineffective, distraught, aggrieved, or some other equally troubling emotion. Frank (1985) suggests that identifying the qualities common to all forms of treatment is crucial. The ways to combat demoralization light the road to hope, skill and renewal. Helping people make useful changes in their *assumptive world* is a central part of the treatment.

The assumptive world is a short-hand expression for a highly structured, complex, interacting set of values, expectations, and images of oneself and others. This assumptive perspective shapes a person's perceptions, behavior, emotional state, and feelings of well-being. One's assumptions help provide order, and predictability (Frank & Franks, communication, 1991).

> The four crucial qualities or conditions Frank's research says are essential for effective therapy include the following:
> 1). an emotionally charged, confiding relationship with a helping person;
> 2). a healing setting that heightens the therapist's prestige and strengthens the patient's expectation of help;
> 3). a rationale, conceptual scheme or myth, that explains the patient's symptoms and that prescribes a ritual or procedure for resolving them, and
> 4). a ritual that requires active participation by both the patient and therapist and that is believed by both to restore health (1985).

Making changes in one's *assumptive world* is a valuable way to understand and strengthen therapy. Demoralization is replaced by hopeful expectations and new strategies to make life better. This deceptively simple formulation argues that an array of different kinds of psychotherapy are viable and effective. When the patient and therapist believe in, commit to, and work together in good faith, the results will follow.

Chapter 7 goes into greater detail about how movies portray therapy, and how cinema can be a useful teaching tool. *A Man for All Seasons,* for instance, depicts a classic conflict involving the powerful influence one person can have on another. Their relationship is a metaphor for therapy. Thomas More's relationship with King Henry VIII was a special example of how one's conscience (shared with another person) creates a powerful bond. Their relationship was a metaphor for therapy. William Glaser (1965) in his book, *Reality Therapy* explains that special bond. Glaser's work has been an effective model particularly with adolescents. We will return to this in the chapter on therapy training.

Consider a few other movies that explore therapy in different ways and settings.

They Might Be Giants (1971). George C. Scott and Joanne Woodward is the woman psychotherapist who treats the retired judge (Scott) for delusions that he is Sherlock Holmes. His brother wants him committed so the family fortune comes to him. The story unfolds with a blend of humor and sensitivity, and leaves the viewer wondering whether or not all delusions are necessarily bad (a theme reminiscent of Don Quixote).

Various *Columbo* movies offer an interesting strategy where the unassuming detective (or a therapist) may take an intentional role (e.g., befuddled, inquisitive, deferring, incredulous). A self-deprecating strategy may prompt people to drop their guard.

Several psychotherapists (e.g., Alexander & French, 1946; Strupp & Binder, 1985) or David Shapiro, 1965) have suggested that the therapist needs to understand, "What role am I being recruited to play?" Discerning this patient's "interpersonal valence," or style, allows the therapist to intentionally take a nonthreatening interactive "role" or relational posture with the patient. This strategy is also known as taking a "transference role." It is a valuable therapeutic strategy to bypass a person's defenses and gather needed leverage. Watching Peter Falk's *Columbo* movies has proven to be a helpful training ground to learn flexibility in gaining influence. Obviously the therapist is not trying to arrest anyone, unless we count trying to arrest self-defeating patterns.

Prescription Murder (1971) or *Murder by the Book* (1967), are just a two of the many efforts this sleuth with the rumpled rain coat, has so classically modeled.

On a humorous note, the movie *What About Bob?* (1991) (with Richard Dreyfus and Bill Murray) portrays the therapist's nightmare patient.
In all fairness Dreyfus may be the patient's nightmare of the shrink with an oversized ego. Murray finds the good doctor's home, meets and is welcomed by the therapist's family. At that point the situation creates some classic comedy situations, as well as a guidebook for what not to do as a therapist.

Cider House Rules (1999). John Irving, Michael Caine, Charlize Theron, Tobey Maguire.

Girl Interrupted (1999). Winona Ryder, Angelina Jolie (best supporting actress). Explores interactions among patients as well as therapy options in a psychiatric hospital circa 1967, outside Boston. It is a good example of how far we have or have not advanced. Borderline personalities of patients mingled with an array of diagnoses among the staff and what the treating culture was like.

Through a Glass Darkly (1961). Ingmar Bergman. Oppressive interactions in a family sharing a holiday on a secluded island focus on a woman recovering from schizophrenia. The players include her husband, her psychologist father and her younger brother. One of Bergman's most mysterious, upsetting and powerful films. Part of the *Silence of God* trilogy, followed by *Winter Light*, and *The Silence*. (Academy Award for best foreign film).

Viktor Frankl (1997) said that the most effective treatment considers three dimensions (medical, spiritual and psychological). These perspectives might even be thought of as, "three rooms" of healing; medical, existential/spiritual and psychological. Psychotherapy is no longer limited to the traditional office setting. Consequently where and how therapy is practiced may have advantages to fixing what "ails us." It is certain, though, that an appreciation of these three dimensions expands the possible ways to change. We revisit this idea in Chapter 3.

Carl Jung's writings on symbols, memories archetypes and dreams (1964, 1965, 1984) provide a way of understanding fears, hopes, and motivations. Understanding dreams and movies offer methods for understanding people, their motivations, puzzles, and solutions for more creative lives.

REFERENCES

Alexander, F., and French, T. (1946). *Psychoanalytic therapy: Principles and applications*. New York: Ronald Press.

Buber, Martin (1958). *I and thou*. New York: Scribner's Sons.

Buber, Martin (1995). *The ten rungs: Hasidic sayings*. New York: Citadel Press.

Capps, D. (1983). *Life cycle theory and pastoral care*. Philadelphia: Fortress Press.

Carlson, R. and Shield, B. (eds.) (1989). *Healers on healing*. New York: Putnam's Sons.

Coles, Robert (1989). *The call of stories: Teaching and the moral imagination*. New York: Houghton Mifflin.

Cooper, Charles (2001). *Personal communication*.
<cooper@hotmail.com>http://www.religiononline.org//cgibin/relsearch ed.dll?action=showitem&gotochapter=6&id.

Cox, M. and Theilgard, F. (1987). *Mutative metaphors in psychotherapy: The aeolian mode*. London: Tavistock.

Dass, Ram (2000). *Still here: Embracing, aging, changing and dying*. New York: Penguin.

Fowler, J. W. (1981). *Stages of faith: The psychology of human development and the quest for meaning.* San Francisco: Harper & Row.

Frank, J. (1985). Therapeutic components shared by all forms of effective therapies. In M. Mahoney and A. Freeman (eds.), *Cognition and psychotherapy.* New York: Plenum.

Frank, Jerome and Frank, Julia (1991). *Persuasion and healing: A comparative study of psychotherapy 3rd ed.* Baltimore: Johns Hopkins Press.

Frankl, Viktor (1973). *The doctor and the soul.* New York: Vintage.

Frankl, Viktor (1997). *Man's search for ultimate meaning.* New York: Plenum.

Gilligan, Carol (1982). *In a different voice: Psychological theory and women's development.* Cambridge: Harvard University Press

Gilligan, Carol, Ward, J. V. & Taylor, J. M. (1988). *Mapping the moral domain: A contribution of women's thinking to psychological theory and education.* Cambridge: Harvard University Press.

Glaser, William (1965). *Reality therapy.* New York: Harper & Row.

Goldstine, D., Larner, K., Zuckerman, S. and Goldstine, H. (1977). *The dance away lover: And other roles wee play in love, sex and marriage.* New York: Ballantine. (Predictable 3 stages of relationships, interpersonal valence: Anxious Ingenue, Disarmer, Provider, Prizewinner, Fragile, Pleaser, Victim, Ragabash, Tough-Fragile.)

Haley, Jay (1990). *Strategies of psychotherapy.* 2nd ed. New York: Triangle Press. Norton & Co. Distributors. (Symptoms as Tactics in interpersonal relations)

Jung, C. (1964). *Man and his symbols.* Garden City, New York: Doubleday.

Jung, C. (1965). *Memories, dreams, reflections.* New York: Vintage.

Jung, C. (1984). *Dream analysis: Bollingen series.* Princeton, NJ: Princeton University Press.

Kimble, Melvin (ed.) (2000). *Victor Frankl's contributions to spirituality and aging.* New York: Haworth Press.

Lazarus, A. A. (1997). *Brief but comprehensive psychotherapy: The multimodal way.* New York: Springer.

Linn, M., Fabricant, S. and Linn, D. (1988). *Healing the eight stages of life.* New York: Paulist Press.

London, Oscar (1996). *Doctor generic will see you now: 33 rules for surviving managed care.* Berkeley, CA: Ten Speed Press.

London, Oscar (1987). *Kill as few patients as possible.* Berkeley, CA: Ten Speed Press.

May, Rollo (1975). *The courage to create.* New York: Norton.

Peake, T. H. (1998). *Healthy aging, healthy treatment: The impact of telling stories.* Westport, CT: Praeger.

Peake, T., Borduin, C. and Archer, R. (2000). *Brief psychotherapies: Changing frames of mind.* Northvale, NJ: Aronson.

Pruyser, Paul (1991). *Religion in psychodynamic perspective.* H. Malony and B. Spilka (eds.) New York: Oxford University Press.

Rogers, Carl (1965). *Client centered therapy.* Boston: Houghton Mifflin.

Satir, Virginia (1988). *The new peoplemaking.* 2nd ed. Mountain View CA: Science and Behavior. (Communication/interpersonal style categories: Distracter, Blamer, Placater, Computer.)

Shapiro, D. (1965). *Neurotic styles.* New York: Basic Books.
Strupp, H. and Binder J. (1985). *Psychotherapy in a new key: A guide to time-limited psychodynamic therapy.* New York: Basic Books.
Tillich, P. (1958). Psychoanalysis, existentialism and theology. *Pastoral Psychology, 9*, 9–17.
Van de Castle, R. (1994). *Our dreaming mind.* New York: Ballantine Books.
Viney, L. (1993). *Life stories: Personal construct therapy with the elderly.* New York: Wiley.
Viorst, J. (1986). *Necessary losses.* New York: Simon & Schuster
Wiesel, E. (1982). *Night.* New York: Bantam Books.
Wulff, D. M. (1991). *Psychology of religion: Classic and contemporary views.* New York: Wiley.
Yalom, I. (1989). *Love's executioner and other tales of psychotherapy.* New York: Basic Books.

4
Dueling Motives: Culture, Gender, and Generation

T. Peake and B. Nussbaum

This chapter samples from a seemingly endless array of cinematic contrasts that haunt us, grieve us, entertain us, and may even enlighten us. The best part is that when done well, these movies force us to look at the issues more closely. Sometimes this fascination is not unlike looking at a train wreck; trying to make sense of it. Sometimes the movies affirm our bias. Sometimes the humor is so bold that the story pierces our defenses and prejudices in ways that force us to think differently. Occasionally we see heroic, enlightened, or inspiring examples of people making sense of difficulty or tragedy. Or sometimes we see people simply making sense.

In training psychotherapists, we have blueprints of predictable stages in life-span development. These were described in Chapter 1. At first we focus on the individual and the challenges that arise with some predictability. When we shift to the family's stages of development we discover that the individual's needs may clash with the family or society (e.g. James Dean's in *Rebel Without a Cause*). Then, the culture, gender, era, or contrasting world views spawn an endless (?) array of plots, puzzles, and possibilities. On the other hand one writer, Polti (1977) has even suggested that there are only *thirty-six* (universal) *dramatic situations*. We will leave that debate unsettled.

One complaint about movies is that they are full of violence, sex, and sleazy values. The sarcastic response would be, "only when done right." Corrupting indeed! But movies also soothe the soul, inspire courage, and offer outlets for aggression and whatever else may ail you. We can try on a few motifs and life strategies that engage, entertain, and enlighten.

There is some caution about lumping people in classifications such as gender, generation, or culture. The labels help organize books, but leave much to be desired when predicting individual taste. That is why it is important to distinguish "which woman [man], in which generation, from which region (culture), in what crisis or what life stage?" These are useful distinctions. The same is true about psychotherapy. A parallel question in planning therapy is, "What patient, with what therapist, in what situation or setting?" Movies can be a good place to practice understanding. We can gain an appreciation for what the characters emotionally "pull," in the viewer or the therapist. The best treatment is usually a matter of knowing and applying the best approach for that person, in their particular situation or life stage. A good match likely produces good results. Cinema offers a wide range of examples to, entertain, plan treatment and foster growth.

CROSS WORLD VIEWS

A Thousand Clowns (1965)
Jason Robards, Barry Gordon, Barbara Harris, Martin Balsam (academy award for best supporting actor).
This memorable movie is adapted from Herb Gardner's Broadway comedy. Jason Robards is a forerunner (without drugs) of the "drop out generation," and the 1960s nonconformists. Robards plays Murray the chief writer for an obnoxious kiddie show. He detests the job but took it (and periodically quits it) in order to enjoy life in New York. His life gets complicated when he becomes the guardian for his young nephew, Nick, and social workers take a dim view of their unique lifestyle.
Some of the funniest lines and situations are captured in the succession of hurdles Murray and the nephew encounter. Examples include Murray's distaste for telephones. He always answers the phone with the same question, "Is this good news or money?" When the caller offers neither, he slams down the phone. Since the social services people cannot reach him, they soon come calling. Another activity the free spirited Murray enjoys is opening his apartment window and yelling out, "Rich people...I want everyone out for volleyball in 15 minutes!"
Murray also allows his nephew to try out different names with the understanding that when he turns 10, nephew Nick will have to decide on a permanent name for himself. The most memorable handle Nick picks for himself is "Dr. Morris S. Fishbein." Murray takes his nephew on lots of funny offbeat outings. They often go to the New York port dock to greet or send-off people on the ocean liners. Murray loves this excitement, since everyone is so happy on these occasions. The fact that they don't know anyone coming or going on the boat is not important. You can imagine how horrified the social services people are when they come to investigate. Barbara Harris plays the woman social worker who gets caught up in Murray's healthy insanity. However, social service officials (Harris aside) demand that Murray must get his act together or lose custody of his nephew. Martin Balsam plays is Murry's brother and agent who tries to get jobs for the free spirit. Murray hates the idea of returning to writing for kiddies show.

Nobody's Fool (1994)
Paul Newman, Melanie Griffith, Jessica Tandy.
Based on Richard Russo's novel of the same name. Another of Russo's novels, *Straight Man*, about the English faculty in a New England college, is just as funny and bittersweet. Paul Newman plays a 60-year-old construction

worker who, in spite of himself, begins to mend an array of broken relationships over the course of the holiday season. The relationships include:

>his grandson and his son; a recently laid off college English teacher,
>
>his nemesis part time employer (Bruce Willis) who has the morals of an alley cat,
>
>Willis' wife (Melanie Griffith) who struggles with romantic possibilities;
>
>a lawyer who constantly tries to get workers' compensation for Newman's mangled leg, injured in an "off the books," accident;
>
>and his landlady (Jessica Tandy)

Tandy's character is the only one who seems to reach his redeemable heart. The ending brings perspective, poetic justice and renewal.

The Trip to Bountiful (1985)
>Geraldine Page, Rebecca De Mornay, John Heard.

This is a superb movie for which Page won the best actress Academy Award. It is set in the mid-1940s in Houston. Cross generational themes are powerful. Mother Watts (Page) lives in a small apartment with her son (Ludie) who works hard to make ends meet after his recent illness. Ludie's wife, Jessie Mae, is every feminist's nightmare, caring little for anything other than beauty parlors, movies, cigarettes, and talking with her lady-friends. Mother Watts wants desperately to return to her home in rural Texas so she can reconnect with the farm, the earth her family tilled, and some proof of her value and generativity. The couple worry about the mother's health, but need her pension income to make ends meet. Mother Watts sings hymns (especially "Softly and Tenderly Jesus Is Mine" by Will L. Thompson) incessantly as a way to affirm and confirm her roots and her worth. Every time the mother sings, the daughter-in-law hears it as an old woman's senility.

Mother Watts escapes and catches a bus for that trip home to Bountiful. On the bus she meets a young woman (Rebecca De Mornay) who is making her own trip back to her parents since her husband has just gone off to war. The women of the two generations learn each other's hopes, fears, confessions, and self-disclosures along the way.

After many surprises on the trip, Mother Watts reaches what is left of her home in Bountiful. The audience comes to appreciate what is lasting in life and something about the meaning of identity, generativity, and integrity. (Horton Foote, who wrote this play, then the movie, also wrote the movie *Tender Mercies* starring Robert Duvall).

Little Voice (1998)
>Jane Horrocks and Michael Caine.

A girl misses her dead father so much that she withdraws from the world and communicates only by singing with the records of Judy Garland, Shirley Bassey, or Edith Piaf. Mom's sleazy talent-agent boyfriend tries to use her as a ticket to money and fame. Little voice clams up when any audience is present.

The Apprenticeship of Dudy Kravitz (1974).
Richard Dreyfuss, Randy Quaid

Dreyfuss plays a young Jewish man in Montreal around 1948. In his quest to "be somebody," he pursues an array of get-rich-quick schemes that backfire in funny and shocking ways. Captures the cultures from which he comes. In one particularly funny episode Dreyfuss has tried to become an avant-garde filmmaker, but cannot get any financing. Reluctantly he films a Jewish wedding and turns the film into an hilariously horrifying sociological venue. He films the traditional shots, but splices films of other cultures such as Samoan and African dances and other rituals like the circumcision *Bris*. You can imagine the reaction of the bride's parents who hired the service.

CROSS CULTURE

To Kill a Mockingbird (1962)
Gregory Peck, Mary Badham, Philip Alford.

Atticus Finch (Gregory Peck), a Southern lawyer, defends a black man, Tom Robinson against the undeserved charge of raping a young poor young white woman. The girl's father should have his picture in the dictionary under the word "bigot."

The story is told through the eyes of Atticus's daughter, Scout. Multiple painful clashes, moral conflicts, and redemption unfold. Few movies have ever captured such a powerful model of integrity in the face of cruelty and bigotry. When speaking to his son after a threatening experience with a drunk; Atticus tells the boy, "there are a lot of ugly things in this world. I wish I could keep them awasy from you, but that's not possible."

A faithful adaptation of Harper Lee's novel; the author based her characterization of the character Dill on Truman Capote: Lee's childhood friend. Peck won the Academy Award for best actor. Robert Duvall had his first movie role (short yet memorable) as Boo Radley, the silent neighbor who saves Atticus from harm.

Guess Who's Coming to Dinner (1967)
Sidney Poitier, Katharine Hepburn, Spencer Tracey.

Controversial in its time, a young white woman brings her black fiance home to meet the parents. A valuable view of the cultural racial climate in the mid-1960's.

Glory (1989)
Morgan Freeman, Matthew Broderick, Denzel Washington.

Tale of the first black company in the Civil War. Based on letters from the white commander Robert Shaw. Denzel Washington won the best supporting actor Academy Award as the firebrand with as much conflicted anger toward his compatriots as he has toward the Southern enemy. It also captures the struggle that they had with their own Yankee troops' acceptance

The night before the biggest battle while the black soldiers are talking, singing, witnessing, and soul-searching about the coming fight, Washington's character calls his brothers "niggers," in a way that captures the strange role they face. In a heated exchange the sergeant, played by Morgan Freeman, confronts and makes it clear, "There's no niggers here!" The next day proves deadly to many of the soldiers both black and white. But a special bond has occurred and the start of an era of upheaval and change.

Spike Lee has created his own movie genre. His movies have been provocative, insightful, but never boring. Lee's niche is far from the historical type Civil War *Glory* film. Rather Lee portrays current cultural realities. Lee gives a voice to crucial themes, with powerful presentations. A synopsis of his contributions is well worth considering.

Do the Right Thing (1989)
A brutal and uncompromising dark comedy about racial tensions in Brooklyn. It is ambivalent in its message as violence erupts, and the lack of a clear message leaves a haunting uncertainty. Stirring questions about causes and solutions. Academy Award nominations for best original screenplay and best supporting actor (Danny Aiello).

Mo' Better Blues (1990)
Joie Lee, Wesley Snipes, Cynda Williams, Denzel Washington, Rueben Blades.
On the surface this is a backstage jazz culture exploration. The apparent theme is a self-interested musician ladies' man, but the racial undercurrents are compelling. Not his most coherent or cohesive work, but the presence of the Branford Marsalis's quartet is compelling. Their music is scored by Lee's father, Bill, on whose life the movie is loosely based.

Jungle Fever (1991)
Wesley Snipes, Samuel Jackson, Halle Berry, Tim Robbins, Tyra Ferrell.
A married black architect's affair with his white secretary creates a backdrop for interracial love. Humor and fresh treatment of the topic. Much of the focus is on the discomfort of friends and relatives, and less on the lovers' challenges. Lee's theme is that cross-race romance is unnatural and never more than skin deep. New York Film Critics Award for best supporting actor went to Samuel Jackson.

She's Gotta Have It (1986)
Filmed entirely in black and white except one powerful scene; some feel this movie put Spike Lee on the map. It is the story is of an independent black girl in Brooklyn and the three men and one woman who compete for her attention. Lee wrote, directed, edited, produced, and starred in the romantic comedy.

Girl 6 (1996)
An aspiring actress (Theresa Randle) takes a job as a phone sex operator to make ends meet. Lots of unusual sub plots as she begins to "take her work home." Relations between work and the world overlap. The story line is not strong, and subplots at times blur. This one has been measured unfavorably against *She's Gotta Have It*.

School Daze (1988)
>Lawrence Fishburn, Ossie Davis. Giancarlo Esposito.
>A rambunctious comedy with a message, set at an African-American college in the South. Fraternities, sororities and themes of keeping or losing the racial/cultural identity are prominent.

Summer of Sam (1999)
>John Leguizamo, Spike Lee, Mira Sorvino.
>Based on David Berkowitz (Son of Sam) and the summer of 1977, when the serial killer terrorized New York City. Focuses on the individuals and the community more than the crimes. As the killer's attacks continue, fear rises along with the temperature. There were notable protests by the families of Berkowitz victims when the movie was released. Lee rarely evades controversy.

Malcolm X (1992)
>Denzel Washington, Angela Bassett.
>A stirring and generally accurate account of the controversial activist and leader for black liberation. While imprisoned in the 1950s Malcolm X hit bottom and then became a Black Muslim and a leader in Nation of Islam. Denzel Washington's performance in the title role brought the movie to a powerful and compelling level. Academy Awards nominations for best actor and best costume design. New York Film Critics Award for best actor.

Crooklyn (1994)
>The focus turns from the life of Malcolm X to Generation X, and the 1970's in Brooklyn.

>Another cultural example (not from Spike Lee) to consider.

Cookie's Fortune (1999)
>Patricia Neal is Cookie Orcutt, the matriarch of a Mississippi small town family with its share of female eccentricities. Cookie "offs" herself to join her dead husband. Her spinster scandal-fearing sister (Glenn Close) hides the suicide note. She tries to shift the blame to the family's loyal good-natured black handyman (Charles Dutton). Comic counterpoint springs from Close's directing a performance of "Salome" at the local church. Cookie's granddaughter (Liv Tyler), is a refreshing, sexually liberated young woman who infiltrates the sheriff's deputy in helping get to the truth of the "non murder." Even the hip country singer Lyle Lovett adds to the remarkable ensemble feel (for which Director Robert Altman is noted).

CROSS WORLD VIEW

Oh Brother Where Art Thou? (2001)
>The Odyssey recycled as Southern America in the 1930s. Won the Academy Award for best musical score. Southern music and prisons, plus the zaniest cast in recent memory.

Blackboard Jungle (1955)
An urban drama about an idealistic teacher in a slum area who fights persistently to connect with unruly students. Bill Hailey's "Rock Around the Clock," was the first use of rock music in a mainstream feature film. See what they started?! Academy Award nominations for best art and set direction, best black and white cinematography, best film editing, best screenplay.

The Milagro Beanfield War (1988)
Ruben Blades, Sonia Braga, Daniel Stern, Julie Carmen, Christopher Walken, Melanie Griffith, Freddy Fender.
Robert Redford's mystical movie based on John Nichol's novel about New Mexican townspeople opposing development. A deceptively simple tale with excellent acting and a mystical pig.. A great launching for other Sundance Movies (Redford's film incubator). Academy Award for best original score.

Angela's Ashes (1999)
Frank McCourt's devastating memoirs growing up poverty stricken with a alcoholic father during the 1930s. The mother struggles valiantly to hold the family together, while dealing with her own depression. A movie guaranteed to make almost anyone feel better about their plight. British Academy Award for best actress (Emily Watson), best cinematography; Academy Award Nomination, Golden Globe Award for best original score.

> An Irish Prayer:
> May those who love us, love us
> And those who don't love us,
> May God turn their hearts
> And if he doesn't turn their hearts
> May he turn their ankles
> So we'll know them by their limping!

Smoke Signals (1999)
Adam Beach, Irene Bedard.
Based on the book, "The Lone Ranger and Tonto Fistfight in Heaven." A geeky orphaned Thomas is reluctantly looked after by Victor (a slightly older also struggling young man of "the Rez") as they try to make sense of their lives, past and future, on an Indian Reservation. A funny, sad, and endearing tale of deep friendship and unvarnished cultural perspective. No gambling casinos on this reservation. The movie won the Sundance Film Festival Award.

> The human brain is not an organ of thinking but an organ of survival, like claw and fangs. It is made in such a way as to make us accept as truth that which is only advantage.
> —Albert Szent-Gyorgi

GENDER THEMES

Women's Themes

When considering movies that motivate, characterize, entertain, and heal women, a resource that stands alone is *Cinematherapy: The Girl's Guide to Movies for Every Mood*. The authors, Nancy Peske and Beverly West, have created and packaged a poignant, insightful, and funny volume that takes the reader to every important theme. It ain't no dry research text, but rather an insiders' guide to girls' (of any age) secrets, joys, hurts, longings, and strategies for love, life and relations. As a bonus the authors squeeze every nuance and wisdom out of the motion pictures they know quite well.

Chapter headings from their book capture the wit and spirit of these creative women:

1. Vacillating between Copious Weeping and Homicidal Rage: PMS Movies
2. Yeah, Okay, So He's a Jerk, But He's Soooo Cute!: Dysfunctional Romance
3. I Hate My Life and I'm Moving to Bora Bora: Seeking Greener Pastures
4. I Know She's My Mom, But She's Driving Me Nuts: Mother Issues
5. But He Has Such Potential, and I Know He Can Change: Earth Mother
6. Going Postal: Working Girl Blues
7. I Just Washed My Hair and I Can't Do a Thing With It: Bad Hair Movies
8. Hell Hath No Fury: Dumped and Out for Blood
9. Someday Has Come and Gone and My Prince Still Hasn't Showed Up
   Happily Ever After Movies
10. I Am Woman, Hear Me Roar: Straining to Hear Your Inner Voice
11. I'm Gonna Eat Some Worms: Martyr Syndrome Movies
12. Nobody Understands Me Like You Do, Girlfriend: Girl's Night Movies
13. When Women Were Women and Men Were Nervous: Men Behaving Well Movies
14. When Men Were Men and Women Were Wicked: Women Behaving Badly Movies
15. My Heart Belongs to Daddy: Father-Issue Movies
16. The Girl Can't Help It: Cult Films Ya Gotta Love

Another pair of resources are also worth mentioning. Oxygen is a television station showing movies and series themes about women. Another channel primarily about women is the Women's Entertainment Network. They use movies on "Cinematherapy." Seven nights a week, actresses Dina Pearlman and Ellen Lancaster portray city women coping with the ravages of life that, "only a movie can cure."

An excellent related book is *Women Who Run with the Wolves: Myths and Stories of the Wild Woman Archetype* (1995). Clarissa Pinkola Este's book is represented well by the movies in the section that follows.

Now and Then (1995)
Four women look back at the girls they used to be in this warm comedy-drama. Author Samantha Albertson (Demi Moore), actress Tina Tercell (Melanie Griffith), gynecologist (Rosie O'Donnell), and housewife Christina DeWitt (Rita Wilson) are friends from childhood who get together for the first time in twenty five years (after their most eventful childhood summer) when Christina is about to have a baby. Seeing the old gang sends Samantha down memory lane, as she recalls the summer of 1970 (their most eventful childhood summer), when the girls were 12 years old and edging into womanhood. Samantha (Gaby Hoffmann) is struggling with the collapse of her parents' marriage. Roberta (Christina Ricci) must deal with the death of her mother. Tina (Thora Birch) is upset over her folks' apparent disinterest in her, and Christina (Ashleigh Aston Moore) is trying to overcome her mother's disinformation campaign about sex.

Thankfully flashbacks comprise three-quarters of the movie. Together, they discuss boys and first kisses, compare notes on the physical and emotional changes they are going through, and have séances where they try to match memory with fact. The younger actresses are talented and charming, adding an enjoyable cross-generational perspective.

Shirley Valentine (1989)
A spirited middle-aged English housewife (Pauline Collins) travels to Greece without her husband and gets a new lease on life. Collins reprises her London and New York theater triumphs on the screen. Via her engaging technique of often turning to the audience to address us, Shirley conveys the internal motives, puzzles, and feelings she considers. A woman's stream of consciousness, and a good film to provoke discussion in therapy, or in teaching therapists the motives and developmental themes that provoke and enlighten.

Crimes of the Heart (1986)
Based on the acclaimed play by Beth Henley we see a few days in the lives of three very strange Southern sisters (or is that redundant?). One has just been arrested for shooting her husband after he ran her black lover out of town. Sissy Spacek is her suicidal sister trying creative ways to "off" herself (e.g., putting her head in the oven) she gives black humor a different meaning. Diane Keaton, Jessica Lange, and Sam Shephard. Won the New York Film Critics' Award.

Thelma and Louise (1991)
Susan Sarandon (Louise) is a hardened and world-weary waitress and Geena Davis (Thelma) the ditzy house wife rebelling against her dominating, abusive, unfaithful husband (who surprisingly provides some of the best comic relief in the film). Brad Pitt is the bad boy who gets Thelma's motor running on this road trip to escape boredom. They accomplish that, but also discover violence and other parts of themselves they never knew. A memorable quote

from this film is: "You shoot off a guy's head with his pants down; believe me, Texas ain't the place you wanna get caught!"

Norma Rae (1979)
A poor uneducated textile worker in North Carolina joins forces with a New York labor organizer to unionize the mill. Sally Field's performance exhibits strength, beauty, and humor and justified her Oscar. Her struggles as a mother, consorter with the Yankee carpetbagger, and her criticism of her home community show timeless issues for women seeking independence without guarantees of support or success.

Bridget Jones's Diary (2001)
Renee Zelweger, Hugh Grant.
The Sharon Maguire film, like the Helen Fielding bestseller on which it is based, captures the hearts of readers like Bridget (Renee Zelweger), who hope to be loved and accepted just as they are. Bridget shows that women don't have to be perfect and rearrange themselves the way the self-help books demand. Hugh Grant plays her love interest as the heroine gains a sense of independence.

Something to Talk About (1995)
One of the funniest scenes in cinema (depending on your perspective). Julia Roberts' husband (Dennis Quaid) comes to call on her after his "tom catting around." The sassy sister-in-law (Kyra Sedgwick) greets Quaid with a swift kick to Quaid's "offending member." Good song's, good laughs, and a great conversation piece.

Sea of Love (1989)
A tough and tightly wound thriller about an alcoholic cop and his midlife crisis. Al Pacino pursues a serial killer, and winds up over his head with Ellen Barkin tying him in knots. John Goodman adds an interesting balance. Sex, anger, and death. No sleeping through this movie.

The First Wives Club (1996).
Bette Midler, Diane Keaton, Goldie Hawn, and Sarah Jessica Parker.
The cast provides a great tale of revenge on heartless husbands and strange tail. Trophy wives, financial revenge with the ex-hubbies' money and a new beginning makes a funny venue for the three lead actresses. Who would be foolish enough to challenge them?

Boy's on the Side (1994)
Whoopi Goldberg, Matthew McConaughey, Anita Gillette, Drew Barrymore, Mary-Louise Parker.
Goldberg is an out of work lesbian singer who connects with a real estate agent for a road trip to California. The pair becomes a female version of the Odd Couple. Barrymore whacks (kills) her drug-crazed boyfriend with a baseball bat, and the entourage are off in what is best described as *Thelma and Louise* coming to *Terms of Endearment* via *Philadelphia*. The popular soundtrack makes the movie stick for a generation that needs passion more than form or message.

Cider House Rules (1997)
Charlize Theron, Erykah Badu, Tobey Maguire.
Based on John Irving's novel of the same name, this movie tackles the realities of love, loneliness, an orphan's innocence, abortion, moral decisions, and coming of age. Set in a Maine orphanage Dr. Larch (Michael Caine) teaches Homer (Tobey Maguire) about: caring for the other children, delivering babies and performing abortions (which Homer refuses). Candy (Theron) shows Homer something of sex and the world. He goes to an apple-orchard (owned by Candy's Dad) where he meets others who struggle with these difficult questions. Academy Award for best supporting actor went to Michael Caine

Driving Miss Daisy (1989)
A sincere and tender portrait of the twenty five-year-old friendship between an aging Jewish woman (Jessica Tandy) and her black chauffeur (Morgan Freeman). The chauffeur is forced upon her by her son (Dan Akroyd). Prejudice in the South, friendship in changing times, and an expanded notion of platonic love. Academy Award to Tandy and nomination for Freeman.

Harriet Lerner's books (*The Dance of Anger, Dance of Intimacy, Dance of Deception*, and others) are listed in the references. Her well-considered perspective has been translated into thirty languages and sold millions of copies. There must be something resonant in her reflections of women's individual and universal themes. A film series on women's issues and Lerner's insights could be an excellent learning experience.

Also two movies which have been reviewed in *The Psychiatric News* (newsletter for American Psychiatric Association) were:

In the Bedroom (2001). This is the powerful story of a couple who's son was murdered by the estranged husband of a woman their son was seeing. The trial did not go well and the husband was released while appeals were dragged out. The combination of rage, angst, and isolation affected both the son's parents and led to desperate measures by the couple.

An Unmarried Woman (1978). This story is the changes that ensue when the woman is divorced by her husband of seventeen years. She goes through the difficult, but predictable struggles of the singles scene, her daughter's sexuality and comes out with a new self-awareness. The movie is unique in that the writer/director puts real people on screen from start to finish.

SEXUALITY AND SOCIETY

The Witches of Eastwick (1987)

"I think...no, I'm positive...that you are the most unattractive man I have ever met in my entire life. You know, in the short time we've been together, you have demonstrated every loathsome characteristic of the male personality and even discovered a few new ones. You are physically repulsive, intellectually retarded, you're morally reprehensible, vulgar, insensitive, selfish, stupid, you have no taste, a lousy sense of humor and you smell. You're not even interesting enough to make me sick."

Cher, as Alexandra Medford, utters those words to the devil (Jack Nicholson) in this shocking and funny film. Cher is joined by Michelle Pfeiffer and Susan Sarandon. "Mad Max" director George Miller meets Hollywood in this rendering of John Updike's novel about three lonely small-town New England women and their sexual liberation. Jack Nicholson is the raunchy overacting, overweight, Mephisto who brings decadent excess to the film. Caution is offered that a bombastic and violent edge to the film may shock or repulse some viewers. However, it is Jack Nicholson's cinematic (if not actual) persona.

Rita Rudner

Rita Rudner (1994) is a unique comedian and movie figure. Her jokes add a lot to the humor of the sexes:

- Men do not like to admit to even momentary imperfection. My husband forgot the code to turn off our burglar alarm. When the police came, he wouldn't admit he'd forgotten the code.....he turned himself in.
- Rich men are often the stingiest. I had one rich boyfriend. When we went out to dinner, I used to order lobster just to watch his pupils constrict.
- Men are very confident people. My husband is so confident that when he watches sports on television, he thinks that if he concentrates he can help his team. If they're in trouble, he coaches them from the living room, and if they're really in trouble I have to get off the phone in case they call him.
- Men who have pierced ears are better prepared for marriage. They've experienced pain and bought jewelry.
- Most men are very difficult to buy presents for. Last year I gave up and handed my father a hundred dollars and said, "Just buy yourself something that will make your life easier." He went out and bought a gift for my mother.
- Men need women. Most single men don't even like people. They live like bears with furniture.
- Men who like foreign films don't eat at Denny's.
- Men who eat at Denny's won't demand a prenuptial.
- Men name their children after themselves, women don't. Have you ever met a Sally, Jr.?
- My husband will cook but not "cook, cook." He'll only barbecue. Men will cook as long as there is danger involved.
- All men look at Dr. Ruth and wonder how she gained all that sexual experience.
- Sumo wrestlers have trouble buying clothing.
- Research has shown that men usually sleep on the right side of the bed. Even in their sleep they have to be right.

Rita Rudner is a low-key (deadpan?) comedian with piercing insight. She made her own movie, *Peter's Friends* (1992), with a focus of the *Big Chill* genre. She invites friends from college for New Years, ten years after graduating. They meet at a grand manor house Peter has just inherited outside London. A sly script and Rudner's comic gifts make it one worth looking for. The quotes above are from her 1994 book, billed as a *Guide to Men.*

Perhaps a few examples of "real" *cross-gender issues* in film would fit here quite well.

Philadelphia (1993)
Academy Awards for best actor (Tom Hanks) and best song "Streets of Philadelphia". Story of a high-powered attorney who is fired when his firm discovers he has AIDS. Criticized by some gay activists as being "too mainstream," it certainly brought the issue to public attention. This movie also includes Denzel Washington (Hanks homophobic attorney), Joanne Woodward, and Antonio Banderas.

Boys in the Band (1970)
A group of gay friends get together one night for a birthday party. A simple premise with a compelling depiction of friendship, lifestyle, and expectations.

My Beautiful Launderette (1985)
An intelligent look at the sexuality, race relations, and economic problems of Thatcher's London. The nephew Omar (Gordon Wamecka) of a Pakistani businessman is challenged to better himself by turning his uncle's rundown laundry into a profitable business. Daniel Day Lewis plays his childhood friend, who is a working-class street punk.

Torch Song Trilogy (1988)
Story of a gay man (adapted from from Harvey Fierstein's Broadway play) who just wants to be loved. Anne Bancroft leads a strong cast (Matthew Broderick, Charles Pierce, Harvey Fierstein).

MEN'S THEMES

Star Wars series summary (1977, 1980, 1983, 1999)

The epic adventure films that comprise the *Star Wars* series are infused with spirituality and love of the human adventurer. The original Star Wars trilogy focuses on a boy named Luke Skywalker and his transition into a young man and finally into a hero of epic proportions. The story may be original, but as Joseph Campbell points out, the theme is thousands of years old. Luke is an immature young man who lives with his aunt and uncle on a farm. He aspires to be a pilot but his guardians do all they can to prevent that from occurring. Luke's adventure begins when his guardians are killed by the evil soldiers who serve the ominous Darth Vader.

Luke begins his journey by meeting with Obi-Wan Kenobi. The older Kenobi possesses powers from an ancient philosophy called the Force. Kenobi quickly becomes Luke's caretaker and teacher. This parallels stories found in many societies about heroes who first learn from older, wiser teacher and then, once strong enough, venture out on their own to right the wrongs of the world. Kenobie represents the ancient Japanese Samurai warriors. Kenobi begins to teach Luke of the Force as they begin their adventure to save Princes Leah from Darth Vader's clutches.

The premise of the first Star Wars saga traces Luke's rise to manhood and his saving of Princess Leah. There is the age-old struggle between good and evil. The two sides are extreme with Darth Vader as the Dark side of the Force who is brutal, murderous, and power seeking. Darth Vader is a tall man outfitted in black with his head covered by mask and helmet. He is feared by his enemies and his followers alike, and uses fear to control every one he can.

What parallels may be drawn here? It is clear that Luke is passing through multiple stages of development as he is abruptly forced out of his role as a farm boy and catapulted into a role of leadership and heroism. This transformation might seem extreme grandiose, because it is. However, Luke's adventure is universal. We take risks, and we get hurt. We strive to achieve personal goals. We face adversity and people who might take advantage of us. We grow, we learn, and we succeed and we fail. Just as Luke did.

Toward the end of *Star Wars: A New Hope*, Luke gains confidence and independence. He begins to trust himself and uses his strengths in a positive way. By this time Kenobi has been killed by Darth Vader, Luke begins to truly realize he has a superhuman gift. He trusts himself with this newfound courage, commitment, and saves his people from slavery and destruction.

The next installment of the *Star Wars Trilogy* is *Episode V: The Empire Strikes Back*. This is by far the most psychologically complex and relevant episode of Star Wars movies to date. Luke is transformed into an icon. He regains his gero status and helps the resistance build a stronghold against Darth Vader and his forces.

Luke is sent to meet with the 900-year-old Jedi master Yoda to learn the ways of the Force. Yoda tests Luke's mind, spirit and eventually agrees to train him. The training is long and includes traditional training in martial arts. Luke learns concentration, commitment, humility, and control. He is tested over and over again by his teacher to prepare him for the temptations of the Dark side of the Force. His training ends when Luke learns that his friends are in trouble, and he leaves to help them.

One of the key elements that Luke learns is how to recognize and suppress libidinal impulses. He commits himself to a way of life, an ethical standard challenged by the Dark side. He learns self-control that his enemies lack. The mentoring Luke receives from Yoda prepares him for the horrors he will face.

The other significant discovery in this episode is that Darth Vader, the second in command of the Dark side, is really Luke's father. Luke faces Vader and is severely wounded when Vader tells the secret. Like Oedipus in the ancient Greek tragedy, Luke is horrified to discover that he has been pitted against his father. Unlike Oedipus, Luke learns this before killing his father. Darth Vader beckons Luke to join him, but Luke resists and retreats. Luke must reassess his strategies and his goal.

The final episode, *Return of the Jedi*, shows a strong-willed adult planning and preparing to destroy the oppressing evil of the Dark side for the last time. Luke is truly a man in this episode. The love triangle between Luke, Han Solo, and Leah is now over as Luke and Leah discover that they are siblings. In addition, Luke's final showdown with Darth Vader changes Vader. He could not kill his own son when commanded to do so. Vader reclaims his parental roles and recognizes the good in his son as a part of himself.

Vader was mortally wounded fighting Luke and the emperor. Before his death, he connected with Luke. Vader and Luke were able to establish an understanding as father and son. Also, Yoda died of old age. The torch had been passed down to the next generation.

As clinicians we do not want to unduly pressure our clients, but we do want them to see the relevance and influence their actions can have. They can see that their life is their own personal adventure. There will be obstacles in the way, and possibly people who would try to benefit at their expense. Part of developing a healthy ego is not succumbing to the "evils" of the world, nor becoming pessimistic or anti-social. We can find different messages in Star Wars. These might include: the triumph of good over evil, an introspective sense of purpose, or a view of ethical responsibility. Thoughtful messages are captured painlessly through the entertainment. Possible areas to include or expand in a clinical class discussion might include: narcissism, the dark side of *the Force* as depression, promoting self-esteem, overcoming phobias, negotiating Eriksonian or Freudian stages, and the paths of therapy and change.

The 2002 *Star Wars* sequel adds to the legacy and the possibilities for future generations.

Other examples of men's themes in film are worth considering.

The Last of His Tribe (1992)

John Voigt (an anthropologist) and Graham Greene (the last *Yahi* Indian) create a masterful study of men from two different cultures. Based on a true story this is the tale of the last Yahi Indian, "Ishi." The professor, Voight (in Northern California), saves Ishi from being killed and then from being sent to a reservation. Ishi becomes an employee of the university and museum. The professor teaches Ishi about the white man's world and sympathizes with him and his losses. Ishi teaches the professor about spirituality, reverence for life, and the eternal circles of earth. This underestimated film has been a favorite in classes we have taught on healthy aging, emphasizing physical, psychological, and spiritual health.

An excellent article by family psychiatrist Frank Pittman (1995) tackles four male leads (Marlon Brando, Paul Newman, Montgomery Clift, and James Dean) at once. In his article, "*Rebels without a Clue,* Pittman weaves a compelling integration using Brando, Newman, Clift, and Dean as the subject of Pittman's brilliant comparison of these four movie giants. They all played (or were?) alienated young men rebelling against society and the demands of the culture that they curtail their passions or angst. They could represent tragic figures romanticized. Part of Pittman's thesis is that none of them (save the later life Newman) made much of their personal lives that might quell the tragic and narcissistic angst. But what movies they turned out!

Marlon Brando: The enigmatic heart throb, tortured soul and now giant (in many senses). His movies included: *The Godfather* (1981). *The Ugly American* (1963), *Apocalypse Now* (1979), *Mutiny on the Bounty* (1962). *Last Tango in Paris* (1973), *A Streetcar Named Desire* (1951), *One-eyed Jacks* (1961), *A Dry White Season* (1989), *On the Waterfront* (1954); to name a few. Brando, who had an alcoholic mother and abusive father, may have outdistanced them with three divorces and reportedly several lovers who committed suicide.

Montgomery Clift: The most neurotic and apparently emotionally pained of the four men. *Red River* (1948), *A Place in the Sun* (1951), and *From Here to Eternity* (1953) were his memorable contributions (plus *Freud*, and *Suddenly Last Summer*). Clift was one of the first male screen stars to pull us into his vulnerable sweet side. Though gay, he never played an openly gay character. He became an alcoholic and after a scarring car wreck, played roles of societal misfits until he drank himself to death at forty-five.

James Dean: With the face of a mischievous angel, a stammering, mumbling style and his vulnerability combined to pull love and protection from women of every age. Dean stole many hearts by dying in a car wreck at twenty-three. His movies, *East of Eden, Rebel Without a Cause*, and *Giant,* remain classics. He defined the tortured adolescent not understood by his father. He may have become the prototype for the tragic hero.

Paul Newman: Pittman (1995) suggests Newman was just as alienated as the other three movie giants, but he appears to be the only one who survived and overcame the tragic-figure alienation. Newman's films include: *The Silver Chalice* (1954), *Somebody Up There Likes M* (1956), *Cat on a Hot Tin Roof* (1958), *Sweet Bird of Youth* (1989), *The Long Hot Summer* (1986), and *The Left Handed Gun* (1958). His next phase featured disenchanted men in: *The Hustler* (1961), *Hud (*1963), *Harper* (1966), and the unforgettable *Cool Hand Luke* (1963). *The Sting* (1973), plus *Butch Cassidy and the Sundance Kid* (1969), gave new meaning to buddy movies with Newman and Robert Redford.

The important difference between Newman and the others is his ability to move into maturity and midlife with some success and perspective. This perspective includes Erik Erikson's adult stages of *Identity, Intimacy, Generativity* and beyond. Newman never makes claims to be a role model. However, he invites us into his struggles (including the well-publicized death of his son, and his charitable foundation that makes good popcorn, salad dressings, salsa, and good will). Newman's more recent movies, *The Color of Money, The Verdict*, and *Nobody's Fool* (Academy Award), give rich meaning to a man's struggle to know himself: to love others and to leave a legacy.

In defense of men who may have "wised up," there is a classic and profound quote in the 1950 movie *Harvey* (about the man who sees and talks to his invisible six-foot rabbit). Jimmy Stewart's memorable line is: "Mom said in this world you must be oh so smart, or oh so pleasant. I tried the first for many years. I'll stick with the second." *Harvey* is another of those movies which makes us wonder who should be the patient.

Men and Women

Can men and women be nonromantic, non sexually involved friends?

"I'll believe it when I see it."
—Jean Renoir, Rules of the Game

"Frankly Scarlet, I don't give a damn."
—Clark Gable as Rhett Butler in *Gone with the Wind.*

When Harry Met Sally (1989)

Billy Crystal, Meg Ryan, and Director Rob Reiner collaborated on the famous and unforgettable "Big O" (orgasm) scene! In a restaurant Crystal told Ryan that women can't really fake a believable orgasm. Ryan captured and commanded the attention of everyone in the room, as she feigned a *world class orgasm*!

A woman "extra" in the restaurant (who was actually Rob Reiner's mother) broke the silence by ad-libbing the famous words, *"I'll have what she's having!"* What do men know?!

One more quote seems somehow relevant here.

"And the lion and the lamb will lie down together, and the lamb won't get much sleep."
—Woody Allen

A caveat about family versus individual development

An important consideration is that individual development theories and applications may be at odds with family stages of development. Erikson's model of individual development is a useful way to chart life-span challenges. However, it is impossible to grasp what a family is (or what emotional and instrumental tasks it fulfills) by simply adding together what is known about each developing person in the family. It is important to examine the interactions that occur and place these demands and themes in a family context. These interactions are governed by implicit rules and are organized to promote internal stability. Just as individuals pass through a series of developmental stages, so the family has a developmental life cycle of its own.

The tasks that a family encounters include: courtship, marriage, childbirth, and dealing with the young, raising adolescents, launching young adults from the home, midlife and retirement, and then old age. Each of these stages involves critical developmental tasks for the family, and stress is usually highest at the transition points from one stage to the next.

There are many good movie examples of such transitions, but one worth mentioning is in the 1980 movie *Ordinary People* (which is also considered in the chapter on training therapists). This family had to face the accidental drowning of one son, along with the suicide attempt of the surviving son. Mary Tyler Moore is an emotionally rigid and cold mother whose personal style and depression blocks the family from grieving. Judd Hirsch plays the wise and engaging therapist who creates a healing environment for the remaining son (Timothy Hutton) to deal with these difficult realities.

The highly regarded family therapist, Gus Napier (1988), makes the funny but true observation that "in every couple each person is trying to 'grow the other one up.' What that really means is that we want to make our partner better at meeting our own needs.

If you want someone to know your lingering, haunting, or inspiring themes, what movies would enlighten them? What would show them the core issues, conundrums, and motivations? How would they fit in Erik Erikson's framework? These questions can guide an exercise in conceptualizing clinical cases and understanding the dynamics, strengths, weaknesses, and developing treatment strategies. Using movies to do it is fun and enlightening. The motif can consider individual, family, cultural, gender, or any challenging issue. Movies can help promote discernment, plus emotional understanding and uncommon sense.

REFERENCES

Chinen, Allan B. (1992). *In the ever after: Fairy tales and the second half of life.* Wilmette, Illinois: Chiron Publications.

Este's, Clarissa Pinkola (1995). *Women who run with the wolves.* New York: Ballantine.

Goldstine, D., Larner, K., Zuckerman, S. & Goldstine, H. (1977). *The danceaway lover: and other roles we play in love, sex and marriage.* New York: Ballantine.

Lerner, Harriet (1997a). *The dance of deception: Pretending and truth telling in women's lives.* New York: HarperTrade.

Lerner, Harriet (1997b). *The dance of intimacy: A guide to courageous acts of change in relationships.* New York: HarperTrade.

Lerner, Harriet (1999). *The dance of anger: A guide to changing the patterns of intimate relationships.* New York: HarperTrade.

Napier, Gus and Whitaker, Carl (1988). *The family crucible: The intense experience of family therapy.* New York: Perennial Library.

Peske, Nancy and West, Beverly (1999). *Cinematherapy: The girl's guide to movies for every mood.* New York: Dell.

Pittman, Frank (1987). *Turning points: Treatment of families in transition and crisis.* New York: Norton

Pittman, Frank (1993). *Man enough: Fathers, sons, and the search for masculinity.* New York: Perigree.

Pittman, Frank (1995). *Rebels without a clue: Screen heroes from the "50's."* Washington, DC: *The Family Therapy Networker* (July, 1995).

Polti, Georges (1977). Translated by L. Ray. *The thirty-six dramatic situations.* Boston: The Writer Inc.

Rudner, Rita (1994). *Rita Rudners's guide to men.* New York: Viking Penguin.

Scarf, Maggie (1988). *Intimate partners: Patterns in love and marriage.* New York: Ballantine Books.

5
Humor, Hungers, and Health

There is a species of primate in South America, more gregarious than most other mammals, with a curious behavior. The members of this species often gather in groups, large and small, and in the course of their mutual chattering, under a wide variety of circumstances, they are induced to engage in bouts of involuntary, convulsive respiration; a sort of loud, helpless, mutually reinforcing group panting that sometimes is so severe as to incapacitate them.

Far from being aversive, these attacks seem to be sought out by most members of the species, some of whom seem to be addicted to them.

> We might be tempted to think that if only we knew what it was like to be them, from the inside, we'd understand this curious addiction of theirs. If we could see it "from their point of view," we would know what it was for. But in this case we can be quite sure that such insight as we might gain would still leave matters mysterious. For we already have the access we seek; the species is *Homo sapiens* (which does inhabit South America, among other places), and the behavior is laughter.
> —Daniel C. Dennett,
> *Consciousness Explained*

Anthropologists have long maintained that the myths each culture transmits to its new members play an important role in shaping their minds (Dennett, 1991, p. 258). Humor and other emotions get good play in the culture of movies.

> Some things are too important to be taken seriously.
> —Oscar Wilde

Silliness? Here are a few candidates to further the cause of health through laughter:

Monty Python's Life of Brian
Monty Python's The Meaning of Life
Monty Python & The Holy Grail

Peter Sellers:

Being There
Dr. Strangelove
*The Magic Christian (*also Ringo Starr*)*
A Shot in the Dark
The Pink Panther
The Mouse That Roared

Steve Martin:

Father of the Bride (I & II)
Leap of Faith
My Blue Heaven
Parenthood
Planes, Trains and Automobiles
All of Me

When hunting for healing humor, be sure to include: Mae West, W. C. Fields, Laurel and Hardy, and the Three Stooges. A positive world view includes a sense of irony or an occasional belly laugh (Seligman, 1991).

HUNGERS AND PRURIENT INTERESTS

What's Love Got to Do With It? (1993)
This story of Tina and Ike Turner tackled the abusive and dysfunctional relation that Tina apparently has more than survived. The movie is a good film to augment therapy. It can be used to teach, or it can be used with patients as a vehicle to focus on the hard parts of dealing oppression and healing.

Pornography

An old psychodynamic adage is that most of humanity's psychological difficulties have to do with sex, anger, and death. The humanists disagree and argue that motives of growth self-actualization are also important. Then, where's the fodder for pornography? Some consideration of what is liberating, what is prurient and what is salacious is worth pursing. Anthropologists have even charted and tried to predict impending wars by the ups and downs of women's skirt or dress hemlines. The professor in the movie, *The Last of His*

Tribe, claimed this rising and falling hemline is no accident. We are not speculating on what is cause and what is effect.

Recently sex addiction has entered the fray as a malady to be treated with its own twelve-step programs (like Alcoholics Anonymous). Classic (or not so classic) lustful cinema, which shocked society at different times, is worth considering. Of course, just for academic reasons you understand.

The Scarlet Letter (1995). Demi Moore, Gary Oldman, Robert Duvall. The classic scandal for many eras.

Red-Headed Woman (1932). Jean Harlow, Chester Morris.

The Pornographers (1966). Bizarre black comedy. A perversely fascinating exploration of Japanese society and the many facets of sexual emotion.

Eyes Wide Shut (1999). Kubrick's last movie. Psychosexual drama. Nicole Kidman, Sydney Pollack, Tom Cruise.

Alfie (1966). The narcissistic male. Michael Caine, Shelley Winters.

Barbarella (1968). Cult classic. Jane Fonda, John Phillip Law, Marcel Marceau.

Emmanuelle (1974). Sylvia Kristel. Filmed in Bangkok.

Looking for Mr. Goodbar (1977). Diane Keaton, Tuesday Weld, Richard Gere, Tom Berenger. Based on Judith Rossner's book of the same name.

She's Gotta Have It (1986) and *Girl 6* (1996). Spike Lee.

Storyville (1992). Southern Gothic New Orleans. James Spader, Joanne Whalley, Jason Robards, Piper Laurie.

Boogie Nights (1997). Burt Reynolds, Julianne Moore, Mark Wahlberg.

Woody Allen once observed that "sex without love is an empty experience, but as far as empty experiences go…it's the best." I believe "prurient interest," is the central concept here.

Sexuality with humor or in the interest of persuasion is an important way to gain perspective. And once again the notion that "some things are too important to be taken seriously" rears its lovely head.

Movies provide a wealth of vivid examples from which to gain a perspective on these troubling yet eternally entertaining sources of pain, pleasure, and puzzlement. Dating back to the ancient Greeks, theater (their movie equivalent) showed the value of catharsis and of influencing the attitudes or culture of the time. *Lysistrata* was one of the most powerful plays of that era in Roman history. The women's strategy was to boycott sex with the warrior males until they stopped there war-making. This play enjoyed a resurrection (some pun intended) of performance during the Vietnam era. During that time of war Americans frustrations with the wrenching "body counts" and updates on the unpopular war appeared on TV news each night at dinnertime.

It's okay to laugh in the bedroom as long as you don't point.

Men are superior to women. They can urinate from a speeding car.

—Will Durst

During sex I fantasize that I'm someone else.
—Richard Lewis

Oysters are supposed to enhance your sexual performance, but they don't work for me. Maybe I put them on too soon.

After making love I said to my girl. "Was that good for you, too?" And she said, "I don't think this was good for anybody."
—Gary Shandling

Instead of getting married again, I'm going to find a woman I don't like and give her a house.
—Lewis Grizzard

Mae West is worth revisiting and quoting for a balance of riveting attention, puncturing pomposity, playful sexuality time-released puns, and the energizing renewal that puts things in perspective.

Too much of a good thing can be wonderful.

I used to be snow-white, but I drifted.

I generally avoid temptation unless I can't resist it.

When choosing between two evils, I always like to take the one I've never tried before.
—Mae West

On a slightly more serious note, Naomi Wolf (1997) wrote an interesting book on promiscuity and the quest for womanhood. No movie available on it yet, but Mae West would probably want to be involved.

THE IMPORTANCE OF POPCORN?

Tastes and satiations: a story in *USA Today* (June 7, 2001) included a study by Screenvisions Cinema Promotions that found that popcorn eaters are three times more likely to cry during movies than those who abstain. Popcorn eaters were also three times more likely to feel romantic. Not a scientific study, but interesting as part of the oral tradition.

Nurturance and the concession stand cannot be underestimated. Kissing in the balcony is an oral passage. Faith Popcorn is another strange social icon whom we cannot seem to grasp, but Andy Warhol would probably have appreciated the connection somehow.

UNREALITY

Here are a few unusual things you might never have noticed about the movies:

It's always possible to park directly outside any building you are visiting.

A detective can only solve a case once he's been suspended from duty.

If you decide to start dancing in the street, everyone you bump into will know all the steps.

Most laptop computers are powerful enough to override the communication systems of any invading alien civilization.

Police departments give their officers personality tests to make sure they are deliberately assigned a partner who is their total opposite.

When they are alone, all foreigners prefer to speak English to each other.

You can always find a chainsaw when you need one.

It does not matter if you are heavily outnumbered in a fight involving martial arts -- your enemies will wait patiently to attach you one by one by dancing around in a threatening manner until you have knocked out their predecessors.

An electric fence, powerful enough to kill a dinosaur will cause no lasting damage to an eight-yea- old child.

Television news bulletins usually contain a story that affects you personally at that precise moment you turn the television on.

A book about psychotherapy, *The 50-minute Hour*, was popular in the 1960s and 1970s. *The 50-minute bladder*, may be a consideration in movie going as the audiences get older.

> There is much to be said in favor of modern journalism. By giving us the opinions of the uneducated, it keeps us in touch with the ignorance of the community.

The only duty we owe history is to rewrite it.

—Oscar Wilde, *The Critic as Artist* (1891)

EMOTIONAL HEALTH AND MIND-BODY THEMES

Emotional Health

To love fully and passionately,
To work at something which brings a fullness of purpose and joy,
and To be able to play as children do.
—Sigmund Freud

> To love well, work well, play well and to expect well.
> —Gerald Caplan

Psychoanalysts are fond of the concepts of catharsis and abreaction. Then the expensive process of "working through" the issues in psychotherapy begins in earnest. Entertainment, insight, reworking and mastery are central concepts in humor, health and mind-body issues. Humor is always part of "playing well."

Mind-Body Themes

Other aspects of emotional and physical health are important to consider, in both prevention, treatment and recovery. There are some valuable principles that guide understanding, treatment and prevention.

> Psychophysiological reconditioning includes *Ego-active* and *Ego-receptive* processes in creativity and in emotional balance.
> —Erika Fromm, A paradox.

We have looked to Erika Fromm (1976, 1981) in several chapters as a master therapist, teacher, and hypnotist who understands and uses states of consciousness in health, treatment, and training as well as on who fosters creativity. Whether we use hypnosis or not; knowing about different states of consciousness help us remember, forget, persuade, and grow. The central idea is that in intentional consciousness we focus and direct our attention. Many tasks require this skill. There is, however, a continuum from focused attention to incidental attention, twilight states and unconscious processes (the opposite of focused attention). Another way to label this spectrum is the range from "ego-active to ego-receptive" thought.

From focusing hard on doing your taxes, to going into deep dream states; might be another way to view the range or spectrum of states of consciousness possibilities. People can be trained to intentionally use states of consciousness to improve health and reduce stress.

Movies take us to different states of consciousness. We can flow through lots of images and immerse ourselves in them. We also talk about left-brain and right-brain processes. Generally the left brain is sequential (digital) and the right brain is simultaneous (analogue). This is said with a number of cautions, but its simplicity helps make the concept clearer. Movies take us through multiple sensory channels. Images (visual, auditory, tactile, gustatory), or music can be used as an "emotional bridge" that travels across our memory without staying on the main highway. Enjoying the processes in movies affects us effortlessly.

Knowing about the processes and the interaction of mind and body can also help us be more creative in therapy and in everyday life.

Soma and Psyche or Mind Body-Themes

This continuum helps: learning, memory, and therapy. These processes can intertwine and affect the autonomic nervous system and it's two dimensions: the sympathetic and parasympathetic functions of that system. Psychosomatic symptoms (which include interactions of physical and psychological causes) such as headaches, ulcers, sleep disorders, Reynaud's disease, irritable bowel syndrome (and a host of others) move in and out of the autonomic nervous system. Knowing about these processes can help plan and apply the best type of therapy.

There are important dimensions in the research literature on mind and body interactions. The treatment of psychophysiological disorders or psychosomatic types of presentations are a fertile ground to understand and promote richer health and happiness. Some important contributors to this specialty include: Herbert Benson (1975, 1979), Ian Wickramasekera (1986, 1988), Wickramasekera, (1996), Davies, and Davis Holmes and Rahe (1967).

These researchers and practitioners can teach us a great deal about the autonomic nervous system. This system is responsible for a number of processes which are "automatic." Breathing, digestion, involuntary muscle contraction or relaxation, blood flow, pupil dilation, and a host of others functions make up the autonomic nervous system. This system has both a *sympathetic* and *parasympathetic* dimension. Response to emergencies (real or perceived) is characteristic of the sympathetic. A calm or more natural state is the parasympathetic domain. When the system is tilted more to an alarm state (for too long a time) the body is at risk to produce symptoms such as headaches, irritable bowel or ulcers, muscle contraction pain, and a host of others. Our health care perspective may be too focused on the acute treatment and diagnostic processes, with only cursory emphasis on prevention. The parasympathetic is characterized by functioning in a calm or usual state free of alarm.

Wickramasekera (1988) wrote a chapter called *"Crocks, Quacks and Shrinks,"* which shows the frustration that doctors may have with patients (crocks) who have these stress-related problems. On the other hand the patients are frustrated with doctors, inability to effectively treat their problems. Consequently the patients view the doctors as quacks. And the aggravation is compounded when the doctors refer the patients to "shrinks" (therapists) who may not be knowledgeable in treating the psychophysiologic type problems.

Good news is here! Herbert Benson has chronicled important ways to understand mind-body interactions and treat such problems with an array of skills in applying the relaxation response (Benson, 1975). Dr. Benson is a professor of medicine at Harvard Medical School and director of behavioral medicine at Boston's Beth Israel Hospital.

The researchers Holmes and Rahe (1967) also did important work in compiling a *Social Readjustment Adjustment Rating Scale*, which helps us grasp the cost of stress and change. Too much change in too little time may put us at risk to develop stress related problems. Prevention or treatment that prescribes an informed way to cope with life stressors can avoid or alleviate these hidden stressors. Much has been done since these earlier works that underscore the immense value of avoiding many medical problems via psychological prevention and treatment.

Also, the popular writer, editor, and scholar, Norman Cousins, in his book (*Head First, The Biology of Hope*; 1989) shares his personal experience and wisdom about mind-body interactions and healing. He emphasizes the importance of laughter and humor as he chronicles his successful recovery from a chronic medical condition. He added movie comedies (including the Marx Brothers) to his treatment regimen.

Another valuable area of research is psycho-neuroimmunology. This emerging science considers the relationship among stress, the immune, and health. Several clinical scientists are integrating new understandings that can stretch this biology of hope (Ader, Felten, & Cohen, 2001; Kemeny & Gruenewald, 2000: and Miller & Cohen, 2001).

An important piece of research with far-reaching implications was done by Follette and Cummings (1979). They demonstrated the preventive value of a course of psychotherapy to reduce medical treatment. This came from a rare opportunity to research and evaluate psychiatric services and medical utilization in a prepaid health care plan venue. These clinicians and researchers were in a unique position to research the benefit of a short course of counseling for people who were "at risk" to develop stress-related medical problems. The researchers had access to the medical history of all the people in the health system. They designed a study where they identified at-risk patients (determined by their health history and other stressors measure by a Holmes and Rahe-type screening). The people at-risk would receive a short course of counseling. A control group of comparable at-risk people did not receive the psychological therapy.

The original Kaiser Permanente Health Care System in California was the setting. This system *was* different than most health maintenance organizations today, in that the medical providers were also the owners of the system. The research from Holmes and Rahe (1967), among others, allowed the clinicians and planners at Kaiser to identify people at risk for developing stress-related problems. The researchers seized the opportunity to provide a short course of psychological therapy to those people at risk. The results showed that the treatment reduced medical utilization by more than 50 percent compared to the control group (also at high risk) who did not get the counseling. Furthermore, the reduction in medical utilization lasted more than three years!

Why, then, is this knowledge not being applied? There are few if any managed care systems now where the owners are the treating professionals. The value of this prevention does not fit with most of our existing insurance systems where a third party (insurance company) usually oversees the allocation of services. This preventive value of psychotherapy is not widely understood or applied. However, the compelling results highlight the benefit of therapy to prevent or alleviate psychosomatic and other stress-related or mind-body maladies. The value of preventive treatment, geared to healthy autonomic nervous system conditioning and prevention, is compelling!

It is difficult to get a man to understand something when his salary
depends on not understanding it.
—Upton Sinclair

At the end of Chapter 1, we told the joke of the seasoned farmer who said, "I don't farm half as well now, as I already know how!" That reality appears in many fields.

LEITMOTIFS

This chapter on humor, hungers and health considers dreams, motivations, compulsions, and ways to prevent, treat, or rise above an array of maladies and aggravations. The processes of analyzing dreams (Jung, 1964, 1965, 1984), has helped the craft of psychotherapy. The world of film provides a universe of "dreams" that show fear, escape, humor, tragedy, perspective, and hope. Movies may unfold like life's realities, ironies, or dreams. Understanding does not always translate into improvement. We can learn patterns that help or harm; but insight does not guarantee improvement in therapy or in cinema. This *curse of insight* comes in therapy and sometimes by watching movies. It is up to us to decide if we use the knowledge for change or purely for entertainment.

REFERENCES

Ader, R., Felten, D. and Cohen, N. (2001). *Psychoneuroimmunology*. 3rd ed. San Diego: Academic Press.

Bandler, R. and Grinder, J. (1976). *The structure of magic: I and II. Books about language and therapy and communication and change.* Palo Alto, CA: Science and Behavioral Books.

Benson, Herbert (1975). *The relaxation response*. New York: William Morrow.

Benson, Herbert (1979). *The mind/body effect*. New York: Berkley Books.

Cousins, N. (1989). *Head first: The biology of hope* (especially the chapter The laughter connection). New York: Dutton.

Dennett, D. C. (1991). *Consciousness explained*. Boston: Little, Brown.

Follette, W. and Cummings, N. (1979). Psychiatric services and medical utilization in a prepaid health plan setting. In *Psychology and national health insurance: A sourcebook*. Washington, DC: American Psychological Association.

Fromm, Erika (1976). Altered states of consciousness and ego psychology. *Social Science Review, 50,* 557–569.

Fromm, Erika (1981). Primary and secondary process in waking and altered states of consciousness. *Academic Psychology Bulletin, 3,* 29–45.

Holmes, T. H. and Rahe, R. H. (1967). The social readjustment rating scale, *Journal of Psychosomatic Research, 11,* 213.

Jones, R. (1970). *The new psychology of dreaming*. New York: Grune and Stratton.

Jung, C. (1964). *Man and his symbols*. Garden City, NY: Doubleday.

Jung, C. (1965). *Memories, dreams, reflections*. New York: Vantage Books.

Jung, C. (1984). *Dream analysis: Notes of the seminar given in 1928–30. Bollingen Series* Princeton NNJ: Princeton University Press.

Kemeny, M. and Gruenewald, T. (2000). Affect, cognition, the immune system and health. In E. Mayer and C. Saper (eds.) *The Biological Basis for Mind Body Interactions* (pp. 291–308). Amsterdam: Elsevier Science.

Miller, G. and Cohen, S. (2001). Psychological interventions and the immune system: A meta-analytic review and critique. *Health Psychology, 20*, 47–63.

Seligman, Martin (1991). *Learned optimism.* New York: Knopf.

Van de Castle, R. (1994). *Our dreaming mind.* New York: Ballantine Books.

Viorst, J. (1989). *Forever 50 and other negotiations.* New York: Simon & Schuster.

Wickramasekera, I. (1986). A model of people at high risk to develop chronic stress-related somatic symptoms: Some predictions. *Professional Psychology: Research and Practice, 17*, 437–447.

Wickramasekera, I. (1988). *Clinical behavioral medicine: Some concepts and procedures.* New York: Plenum.

Wickramasekera, I., Davies, T. and Davies, S. (1996). Applied psychophysiology: A bridge between the biomedical model and the biopsychosocial model in family medicine. *Professional Psychology: Research and Practice, 27*, 221–233.

Wolf, Naomi (1997). *Promiscuities: The secrets struggle for womanhood.* New York: Random House.

6
Generational Resonance: To Era Is Human, to Forgive, Divine

One generation's treasured themes may have no meaning (or even an aversive meaning) to children of another era. Tom Brokaw's book *The Greatest Generation* may be off-putting to current "30-somethings" while inspiring to the "50-something" generation who are the children of World War II. It is important to understand what themes capture the hopes, fears, irritants, and inspiration of other generations. The silver screen conveys and resonates those eras and memories. Movies can foster insight, empathy, inspiration, and growth to bridge generational disparity. That benefit is entertaining, but also a way to connect.

In his research, Sehulster (1996) noticed that a person's identity can be explored or understood through that person's favorite films or books. People perceive their sense of self through memories of a special time or era. He even developed a way to interview people about their memories and movie preferences in a way that highlights their sense of self or a defining era. These special memories can shape or affirm the core of who we are, and what we can become. Not surprisingly the cherished themes of one generation may have little, or even annoying, meaning to another.

Pivotal movies that anchor each generation's or cultures shared history (and social challenges) can be a good way to bridge differences. *Agecohorts* is a sociological concept to help understand the influential historical or social events for different eras. Appreciating these can give helping professionals a real advantage in rapport and credibility. That doesn't mean we have to know it all, but our sincere curiosity amplifies the trust and climate so people can "think out loud," about pivotal hopes and fears.

The dimensions are endless. Shared humor, struggle, shame, loss, pride, and renewal play well in cinema and narrative history.

Consider some movies by decade or shared eras. A few representative examples are worth considering.

1910–1920s

Birth of a Nation. (1915). This lavish Civil War epic was the first feature length film (silent) and brought credibility to the industry. D. W. Griffith wrote the screenplay, directed it, and set it to a musical score. Based on the play, *The Clansman*, and a book, *The Leopard's Spots* (Thomas Dixon); *Birth of a Nation* depicts some of the most moving scenes ever created. The film is of great historical significance (Griffith's positive attitude toward the KKK notwithstanding).

1930s

All Quiet on the Western Front. (1930). The tragedy of World War I unvarnished.

It Happened One Night (1934). An antagonistic couple determined to teach each other about life, via screwball comedy.

1940s

How Green Was My Valley (1941). In a fifty-year span of Welsh culture, director John Ford captures the range of challenges, tragedy and triumphs.

Casablanca (1942). War, love and sacrifice. Humphrey Bogart and Lauren Bacall.

All the King's Men (1949). The Depression's problems focused on Huey Long's Louisiana, corrupt life, and style.

1950s

All About Eve (1950). Bette Davis offers new possibilities for women's roles.

On the Waterfront (1954). Who are the heroes and who are the villains?

1960s

West Side Story (1961). Cultural tribes and tragedies set to music.
Midnight Cowboy (1969). Dark desperation and friendship.

1970s

Annie Hall (1977). Neurotic anxiety, love and our humorous traits.
The Deer Hunter (1978). Questioning whether God is on our side.

1980s

>*Ghandi* (1982). The meaning of love and generativity.
>*Rain Man* (1988). Uniqueness and caring versus the "me generation."

1990s

>*Dances with Wolves* (1990). Reconsidering America's identity.
>*Unforgiven* (1992). Reconsidering the cowboy's villain archetype.
>*Shakespeare in Love* (1998). Rewriting our myths and poet archetypes.

OTHER THEMES?

Movie genres of humor evolved from the 1930s to 1950s and beyond, via such comedy groups or comedians as:

>Laurel and Hardy (1920–51)
>The Little Rascals (1929–50s)
>The Three Stooges (1950–60s)
>Bowery Boys (1940–50s)
>Abbott and Costello (1940–50s)
>Charley Chaplin (1914–50s
>Lucille Ball (1930–70s)
>Bob Hope (1930–70s)
>Red Skelton (1930–60s)
>Peter Sellers (1952–80s)
>Dean Martin and Jerry Lewis (1949–60s)
>Walter Matthau (1950–90s +)
>John Belushi (1970s)
>Dan Akroyd (1970–80s)
>Bill Murray (1970–2000s)
>Robin Williams (1977–2000s)
>Cameron Diaz (1994–2000s)

Tastes in humor are both era-specific and eternal. Our apologies if your preferences are missing, but that may inspire your own examples.

The Marx Brothers had a hand (and some funny walks) in shaping culture as well. The brothers had honking horns, outrageous walks, and made "clang associations" something to laugh at rather than a symptom of schizophrenia. The brothers created great relief and perspective to cope with too much seriousness.

>Consider a few:

>*The Cocoanuts* (1929)
>*Monkey Business* (1931)
>*Horse Feathers* (1932)

Duck Soup (1933)
A Night at the Opera (1935)
A Day at the Races (1937)
Room Service (1938)
Stage Door Canteen (1943)
A Night in Casablanca (1946)
Love Happy (1950)
The Marx Brothers in a Nutshell (1990)

And the humor goes on.

National Lampoon's Animal House (1978)
A true generation-anchoring film. Set in 1962, the resonance of Vietnam, eternal adolescence, and poor taste hit the now "50-somehting" baby boomers in their funny bone. John Belushi runs amuck, and "road trip movies" are granted a place in film for years to come.

The Truth About Cats and Dogs (1996)
A horse of a different color or era. Janeane Garofalo, Uma Thurman and Ben Chaplin, star in this funny movie that blends cat/dog people distinctions with men/women distinctions. It also gently introduces the idea of phone sex to the uninitiated. Thurman is sweet, sexy, and terminally obtuse. Garofalo's observations on men and love are woven in ironic, biting and funny ways. Chaplin's character thinks the wise Garofalo's character can come in the sultry Thurman package.

Cross-generational examples in cinema may also have enduring messages. Consider a few movies that capture the fascination, angst, sorrow, hope and core fears and philosophies of the 60–80-year-old generation. Some examples are offered.

ROBERT ALTMAN AS AN ICON AND SOCIAL SHAPER AND COMMENTATOR

In an article by Andy Seiler (*USA Today*; 1/4/02) we are refocused on the work and thoughts of filmmaker Robert Altman. Evidently one of Altman's observations was that, "It's all video now." People see movies between their feet (especially grown ups). A generation has grown up with a number of his prize-winning movies.

Altman has at various times been blamed for: undercutting our military efforts (in Vietnam via *M*A*S*H*), the murder of John Lennon (a famous singer was assassinated in Altman's film *Nashville*), and condoning drug use.

M*A*S*H (1970). Altman launched sophisticated rock and roll cinema and captured the Vietnam era. The TV spin off made sure more than one generation has the prototype imbedded in the brain.

McCabe and Mrs. Miller (1971). An entrepreneur opens a brothel in the Great North.
Nashville (1975). A political campaign/music festival in Nashville.
The Player (1992). A grand satire of the movies' industry and its greed.
Gosford Park (2001). A social satire with a mystery focus and the ensemble cast that Altman has so often used to great advantage. Most actors consider his movies as the equivalent of a family village atmosphere. Lots of village characters and idiots (in the best meaning of the word).
California Split (1974). A comedy about compulsive gambling, with George Segal and Elliott Gould.
A Wedding (1978). His weakest work.
Kansas City (1996) Jennifer Jason Leigh and Harry Belafonte star in this 1930s period movie about jazz, robbery, abduction and an FDR advisor. This film has great music and is a good example of an "age cohort," movie.
Dr. T and the Women (2000). A hysterical comedy about the subculture of rich and pampered Texas women and Richard Gere as a gynecologist in a midlife crisis.

Altman has a gift for capturing the feel and issues of different eras. His subject matter spans an interesting array of generations; at times using history to paint current eras in a new light.

Judith Viorst wrote a book called *Necessary Losses*, which explains that changes across life stages represent both loss and growth. That applies to individuals, but also to cultures and societies. Shared experiences provide a bond and a basis to relate. They also help us transition through cultural as well as personal life experiences. The tragedies of New York, September 11, 2001, will shape our lives and views for years to come.

As mentioned before, Sehulster (1996) wrote an interesting article on the memories people have of special shared experience or eras. The vivid associations can be discovered by asking people to highlight movies or books that remind them of times that changed them.

Consider wars and financial markers, such as the stock market crash of 1929. The spirit of the times or "zeitgeist," is another way of considering cultural influences. There is an interesting observation by the professor/museum curator in the movie *The Last of His Tribe*, about skirt hems, the economy and war. He suggested that women's hemlines are shortest after wars. The professor didn't give us the explanation for what causes what.

Tom Brokaw's book, *The Greatest Generation,* gives us a heart warming example of the strength and conviction of people from the World War II era. The aftermath of that ordeal was captured in *Judgment at Nuremberg* (1961). This classic offered perspective and an opportunity for a country and the world to reconsider the ordeal that shook the globe via World War II. Marlene Dietrich, Burt Lancaster, and Spencer Tracy played memorable roles in the war crimes trial. Director Stanley Kramer brought his prowess to this important venue.

On the other hand not all older adults are so positive. Gordon Livingston, a psychiatrist in Columbia Maryland, writing for the *San Francisco Chronicle* (8/26/01), offered some examples of seniors who become whiners.

Although one of the risks we run through life is to become a cultural cliché, such as rebellious teen, naive newlywed, the conspicuous consuming yuppie, or the indolent retiree. Following up on that notion, Gordon offers some recommendations if you're granted longevity.

    Stop complaining. A couple of generations earlier, you'd have been dead for 10 years.
    If you have more than 10 doctors' visits a year and don't have a terminal illness, get a new hobby.
    If you don't have an activity that causes you to lose track of time, you need one.
    If anyone wants to know what life was like when you were their age, they'll ask.
    It's true no good music has been written in 30 years. Neither your children nor your grandchildren want to hear about it.
    Courage is ageless. Relinquish dignity last.

    The *Sandwich Generation* is a recent label for baby boomers pulled and stretched between their parents and their children. Mary Pipher's (1999) book, *Another Country*, is a valuable resource about this emotional terrain.
    What's "hip" per generation? The drive-in theater was its own culture and created lasting effects (besides accidental pregnancies), which defined an era and shared experiences that make age cohorts.
    From prohibition, avant-garde phases, beat-nicks, martinis through psychedelia, ecstasy to latte. One could even anchor "drugs of choice," per various generations.
    What's enduring? Adolescence may be an enduring state of mind. It is worth considering some Jungian archetypes such as the concept of *puer eternis* or "the eternal adolescent," (Stevens, 1990). This spirit may endure in every age or generation. Will we ever grow up?
    More recent versions adolescent issues include *Girl Interrupted* (1999). Angelina Jolie and Wynona Ryder are patients in a psychiatric hospital. Although a current movie, the story is set in the 1960s but has strong appeal to current adolescents and 20-somethings.
    Pretty in Pink, *Grosse Point Blank*, *Breakfast Club*, *Risky Business*, and *Something About Mary*, are other examples of today's adolescents. However we do know that every age can savor their own favorite or enduring life stage.

    Also, regional flavors mix well with eras. An interesting magazine with a Southern flavor (*Oxford American Magazine: The Southern Magazine of Good Writing*) dedicated an issue to Southern movies, movie makers, and movie writers. One of the favorites was Billy Bob Thornton's *Sling Blade* (1996). It won an Academy Award for best adapted screenplay.
    In application, we have had great success in doing groups with people of all ages, by asking them to consider the decades of their lives and then list situations that stand out in their memory of those times. The process engages people well, while also helping them understand and reclaim resources that have helped them navigate past challenges. This is a variation on the William James

quote: "We learn to swim in the winter and to ice skate in the summer." Using movies with shared generational, geographic, cultural themes and sentimental memories may provide even stronger participation in training therapists or in doing therapy. Encouraging therapist students, clients, or friends to identify their cherished or haunting issues, eras or themes; is a fun and enlightening endeavor.

REFERENCES

Brokaw, Tom (1998). *The greatest generation.* New York, NY, Random House.

Chinen, Alan (1989). *In the ever after: Fairy tales for the second half of life.* Wilmette, IL: Chiron Publishers.

Kaufman, Sharon (1986). *The ageless self: Sources of meaning in late life.* WI: Madison, University of Wisconsin Press.

Livingston, Gordon (August 26, 2001). San Francisco, CA: San Francisco Chronicle.

Pipher, Mary (1994). *Reviving Ophelia: Saving the selves of adolescent girls.* New York: Grosset/Putnam.

Pipher, Mary (1999). *Another country: Navigating the emotional terrain of our elders.* New York: Riverhead Books.

Sehulster, J. R. (1996). In my era: Evidence for the perception of a special period of the past. *Memory 4,* 145–158. (Psychology Press, an imprint of Erlbaum. Taylor and Francis Ltd.)

Seiler, Andy (January 4, 2002). Robert Altman's Film Legacy. McLean, VA: U.S.A. Today.

Southern Movie Issue: (2002) *Oxford american.* Special Edition. Winter Issue, #42 (ISSN 10744525). Oxford, MS: , John Grisham.

Stevens, Anthony (1990). *On Jung.* London: Penguin Books.

Viorst, J. (1986). *Necessary losses.* New York: Ballantine.

Wedding, D. and Boyd, M. (1999). *Movies and mental illness: Using films to understand psychopathology.* New York: McGraw-Hill.

7
Training Therapists: Hearing, Discerning, and Revising Life Stories—Using Images Generated from Valuable and Favorite Movies

How can a budding or (or previously bloomed) therapist use this book to develop, strengthen, renew, or expand her/his comfort, acumen and skills in doing therapy? The best way is to create a climate where people feel free to tell their story. The gift is to hear, discern and help people revise the chapters of their lives that need reconsidered or rewritten. This is not so much a manual for how to do therapy, but rather an attempt to help therapists (at any stage of their development) to appreciate the importance of knowing, honoring, and conveying the dimensions of person's life journey. A guiding them is the *minimal interference principle*. This principle attempts to recognize the strengths, challenges, and current plight that a person, couple, or family may be facing. When using this strategy we strive to find out how the person has navigated life challenges at earlier times, and what kind of problems they may be facing now. People tend to come to therapy at a time when they are demoralized. Rather than start the process trying with a major overhaul, we search for a person's strengths or ways they have navigated past challenges. In the 1960s and 1970s it was common to hear patients say they needed to "find themselves." Probably that phrase was more prevalent on the West Coast when therapy was king in California. The easiest way to build on past successes or strengths' is to ask and find out "When did you last have yourself?" Think of a person's identity as being an exercise in telling one's life story. Times of problems may be thought of as a person's life story "going awry." And therapy can then be an exercise in life story reconstruction. Make no more changes than necessary, but build on past strengths to combat demoralization and rewrite the necessary chapters to restore a hopeful outlook with strategies to face the demands of current life stages.

One enduring psychological diagnostic tool across several decades is a "projective" test called the: *Thematic Apperception Test*. This procedure takes about ten pictures (there are actually more to choose from) and asks the client to tell a story about the pictures.

"There is no right answer. But tell what the people in the picture are doing, what they are thinking or feeling; and how the story will turn out." The stories are deciphered by identifying:

> 1). a need or needs that are expressed in the stories;
> 2). the "press," (which includes the environment or people the client; feels help or hinder the client meeting their needs), and
> 3). the storyteller's imagined outcome (good, bad, etc.). How will it turn out?

Repetitive themes, needs, dilemmas, or solutions are extracted via this process. Obviously, themes that appear often in the stories provide a window to one's hopes, fears, motivations, and perspective.

Movies can serve this same function, vicariously providing a practice field to mourn, celebrate, understand, feel, and escape or master life's challenges. Movies may also be like folk tales from different cultures. If so, their archetypal value offers guidance through the entertainment and perspective. A book by a psychiatrist Allan Chinen (1989) *In the Everafter: Fairy Tales and the Second Half of Life*, is a compilation of folk tales from different countries. His book suggests that elders are highly valued in many cultures, but America has very few stories that honor seniors. Rollo May (1991) offers the classic story of Peer Gynt as an example of a man's problem in loving. This tale provides a good place to practice understanding and motivation.

Another approach is through dreams and their analysis. Carl Jung (1984) provides a rich legacy that draws from an array of personal or universal themes. Chinen draws heavily from Jung. Jung's method discerns repetitive themes, hopes and fears; as well as identifying existing strengths and strategies. Jung's enduring contributions provide an interpretive strategy. He considers cultural and universal (archetypal) dilemmas that people face. Jung points us toward processes such as: *reversal, imago, collective unconscious, and the shadow,* that expand the range of resources. Joseph Campbell (1988) and Christopher Vogler (1998) mentioned in earlier chapter's, have made Jung more accessible. They show how Jung's psychology discovers a *deep structure* characteristic of enduring universal themes.

There is a saying that "when we are stressed (and need to be the most creative), we may be the least creative." This pattern is called the "neurotic paradox" (Mowrer, 1953).

This chapter looks at an array of concepts, adages, principles, cautions, and trip-wires in learning to do psychotherapy. We propose central qualities that make "the talking cure" effective. A rich array of movies is available. Good therapy may include growing, grieving, renewing, and reviving a robust hopefulness. Movie examples from which to draw are plentiful. However, "shrinks" in movies are often portrayed in the worst light. An old saying is that, "Some people's role in life is to serve as a bad example." Perhaps we can make a stab at distinguishing between the good, the bad and the ugly.

CAVEATS

> You start graduate school with a thirst for knowledge. Then we attach your mouth to a fire hose."
> —anonymous professor

> Be careful of reading health books. You may die of a misprint.
> —Mark Twain

PREDICTABLE STAGES IN DEVELOPMENT AS A PSYCHOTHERAPIST

There is a sizable literature that describes predictable processes or a sequence of stages that psychotherapists go through in their own development and maturation as effective professionals. This evolution is not chronicled in movies, as far as we know. However it is worth considering, because movies can be used in helping train therapists to understand their own reactions, feelings, and the emotional "pull" or valence that certain patients or situations provoke.

Several psychologists and psychiatrists who teach and supervise psychotherapists have explained "predictable stages" or passages that evolve in "learning the trade" (e.g., Doehrman, 1976; Friedman & Kaslow, 1986; Hess, 1980; Ralph, 1980; Archer and Peake, 1984). One basic model of therapist evolution, by Ralph, chronicles four phases. The *first stage* is the novice clinician who learns the role of therapist as a nondirective expert. In this phase the task is gathering information that leads to a diagnostic understanding. Here the mindset is similar to a medical model of making an accurate diagnosis. However, in psychotherapy, diagnosis does not always prescribe a single treatment strategy (as happens in medicine). The therapist does not just "treat," but is also a collaborator who involves the patient in the process. The *second stage* is where the therapist adopts a theoretical approach in a concrete fashion and "tries on" this model or strategy with the client. Some therapy trainers have jokingly suggested the novice therapist shows the conviction of a new missionary or religious convert. Different "denominations" can be sampled along the way. The student therapist understandably looks for concrete guidance with a promise of certainty.

The *third* and *fourth* stages differ from the first two by introducing the concept of the patient-therapist *process*. The *relational process* (in contrast to just the *content*, complaint, or topic of therapy) is both crucial and intriguing. In this relational dimension, an important question for the therapist is, "What role am I being recruited to play?" The patient carries an interpersonal style into relations. Or stated another way, "What does this patient *pull in me*?" In the third stage Ralph (1980) says there is a shift to a "relationship centered focus." Recognizing and understanding this interpersonal style is crucial. The concept of transference (the client's way of relating to and feelings about the therapist) and counter transference (what the client "pulls" emotionally in the therapist) are a rich and intriguing dimension in changing people. Not just behavior changes, but a new awareness of one's *interpersonal impact* and style of relating; can offer new freedom, new responsibility; and new options.

The fourth stage is more focused on making sure the therapist keeps him or herself healthy by watching for "blind spots" or emotional prejudices (or over investment) that could interfere with treatment. This stage has prompted many schools of therapy (family therapy and psychodynamic training programs) to encourage personal therapy for the therapist as part of training, and as a periodic tune-up during the course of one's career.

THE MINIMAL INTERFERENCE PRINCIPLE

In Chapter 2 we previewed the *minimal interference principle*. This means that when helping people in psychotherapy we should make no more changes than necessary. Learn and honor the identity a person has created while discerning facets that are not working. At times the author has had patients come to therapy saying that they need to find themselves. The crucial question to ask is where/when did you last have yourself? Stress, life changes, and loss can make us self-defeating and creatively dumb. To practice the minimal interference principle we must truly honor and understand the person's identity and the situations that support or attack one's sense of self. Pressures from insurance and managed care heighten the need to work quickly yet effectively. The art of telling, revising and rewriting lives applies this "make the least change necessary" principle.

A person or family's identity is an exercise in telling a life story. Times of troubles are instances of life stories gone awry. And therapy can be thought of as an exercise in story repair. Movies help us immensely to gain perspective about situations that vex us. In stressful or emotional times our stress, over involvement or other blind spots keep us from seeing or creating a new strategy or solution. Cinema offers emotionally charged recognition, but also a safe distance from the pressure so we can plan with perspective. This personal recognition allows us to: laugh, cry, grieve, understand and provide an opportunity to rewrite our lives. Movies also give us a vehicle to make a connection with other people, and thereby hash and rehash the problems, comedies, successes and necessary losses that provide new insights, choices and strengths. Lest we get too serious, movies can provide a fun or a helpful escape when we've been thinking too hard already. Remember. "some things are too important to be taken seriously."

The In Laws (1979)
Peter Falk, Alan Arkin.
This is a wild comedy to help the beginning (or experienced therapist) test their mettle. Falk claims to be a CIA agent. Alan Arkin is a dentist whose daughter is marrying Falk's son. The fathers end up foiling a South American dictator's counterfeiting scheme. The hilariously convoluted plot guarantees a challenge in discernment with a side order of recognizable family pathologies. Now this is the way to learn therapy and family process from a distance without danger of personal injury.

Mottoes and Core Dynamics

In training therapists there are many skills to be learned (as well as facts and classifications). We talk about core qualities, central motivations or prominent strivings. Teaching practitioners to recognize, feel, and appreciate their patients condition is crucial. Learning to listen for these core dynamics can draw heavily on time honored human stories. The important parallel is the similarity between living central human stories, and developing the ability to feel and capture people's hopes and fears.

In movies we can trace the central plot (most times). Seeing that plot structure, is important. The skills needed to grasp and convey the defining personal struggle (or core dynamic) of the patients we treat, has much in common with the wisdom of good cinema.

Cinema also gives us good examples of a number of strategies for change (also sometimes called mutative processes), like affective bridges, hypnosis, conscious and unconscious understanding, and the *curse of insight*. These and others techniques promote growth and pivotal change in people's lives.

Sometimes movies let us create new understandings; and sometimes they let us just plain play. New perspectives on old problems often occur when we can laugh freely.

Core Qualities: Frank Conclusions

Jerome Frank (often touted as one of the most influential writers on, and practitioners of psychotherapy) and his daughter Julia (both excellent psychiatrists) collaborated on a third edition of his book, *Persuasion and Healing*, which tackles the similarities of psychotherapy to other forms of human change. They treat topics ranging from religious revivalism and magical healing, to contemporary psychotherapies, from the role of the shaman in non-industrialized societies to the traditional mental health hospital. The third edition of this book offers information on self-help, family therapy, psychopharmacology, psychotherapy for medical conditions, and techniques such as bioenergetics and primal therapy.

Frank and Frank's (1991) reflection on the shared components of effective psychotherapy include:

> 1). an emotionally charged, confiding relationship with a helping person;
> 2). a healing setting that heightens the therapist's prestige and that strengthens the patient's expectation of help;
> 3). a rationale, conceptual scheme, or myth that explains the patient's symptoms and that prescribes a ritual or procedure for resolving them; and
> 4). a ritual that requires active participation by both the patient (or couple, family, etc.) and therapist that is believed by both to restore health.

Effective therapies share a common element: to "combat the sufferer's demoralization." Therapy must be "hope engendering." Many therapies are surprisingly similar to rhetoric (the art of persuasion) and hermeneutics (the study of meanings). In an earlier version of the book, Frank even examined brainwashing (he elected not to suggest this strategy). His unique approach, mixed with scholarly and empirical examination (even anthropology, at times) describes the core of valuable change. Healing rhetoric and the core qualities of change, strengthen the ties among the various healing professions. Frank opened the door to cinema, music, poetry, literature, and friendships as additional paths to growth and healing.

The uses of enchantment, as described by Bettelheim, (1977) is a metaphor to help us discover and use skills to entrance, captivate, and change peoples' perspectives. Core dynamics (which we have also called life bets, core beliefs, leit motifs, attributions, fears, and fascinations) are like the story line, plus the challenges that people face. Movies can leave us bemused, bereft, bewildered, bewitched yet they can lead us to solutions. There is a difference between habitual and intentional behavior. A good bit of good psychotherapy is "making the unconscious…conscious." Or put another way, by giving someone the "curse of insight," we can hold them responsible to see a pattern and know they can change it to their benefit. A collaborative approach with clients gives them insight and ways to change their strategies. In this way they can exit self-defeating patterns.

These are a few of the advantages, strategies, or skills that movies can help therapists hone by learning to read the essential themes and motivations. Sometimes we can help people who have been struck dumb (rendered ineffective by stressors or losses) to be struck smart (understand the stressors) and rewrite their stories.

In teaching psychotherapists for many years, we have found a common puzzle or question for new therapists is, "when are we through?" Managed care (or what some therapists jokingly renamed "mangled care") is an effort to have a third party govern the length of therapy. Even with someone looking over our shoulder, there are good metaphors to help people benefit in a shorter course of counseling. One analogy for this is to think of the psychotherapist as being like a family doctor who makes interventions at "symptomatic junctures," across the life span. In order to do this effectively it is crucial to be able to interview and assess patients in a thorough fashion, so we come to know their "core dynamics."

As we come to know them and create a trusting and safe environment, we help them understand their problems, causes and potential solutions. When their life gets on the wrong road we can provide perspective and options to get back on track. As one patient humorously observed: It's like the old Vaudeville routine. You tell the doctor, "It hurts when I do this." Then the doctor hits you with a rubber chicken and says, "Don't do that!"

Sometimes therapy has been described as helping people "find themselves." The most parsimonious strategy is to figure out when they "last had themselves," and reclaim or rebuild the confidence challenged by current stressors or losses. The quality of the relationship is crucial. The commitment and confidential dimension are also essential to help people understand the pattern and try new solutions.

The *curse of insight* is also an important concept. Not all patients are highly motivated nor are they sincerely invested in change. In psychiatric nomenclature we label some people as "character disorders," or personality disorders. This often means that they are not interested in changing. Usually the other people in their lives are the ones who beg for them to change. The most effective therapist cannot guide or motivate them to change or strive for self-improvement. Movies are full of these characterological characters. They make for entertaining drama. But in real life they are no fun (come to think of it that may depend on your diagnosis). So, in these situations, the best strategy is to point out their style (core pattern) and their impact on others. Make them aware of the cause and effect, and lay out a tight structure that gives you the leverage to force change. Or if no change occurs, then your description of their pattern will haunt them as *the curse of insight*! Addictive people, con artists, "borderline personalities" (think Glen Close in the movie *Fatal Attraction*) and career felons are some examples. These patients generally fall under "AXIS II" diagnosis categories or what are also called *personality disorders*. A popular notion is that politics might attract a few such characters.

Even in less extreme examples, the curse of insight is something that gives any client a new perspective about inadvertent patterns of their behavior. Once the problem, the puzzle, the cause-and-effect, the triggers are know, new strategies can be tried in the safe surrounds of therapy. Then they can be applied to real life situations.

Causal schemes in therapy may be straight or divergent lines, systemic interactions, or paradoxical themes, to name a few. A range of theories and skills help us understand the "hopes and fears" that guide behavior. Polanyi (1966) in his book, *The Tacit Dimension*, describes the craft of psychotherapy with concepts like tacit knowing, prescience and indwelling. Carl Roger's client-centered therapy was influenced by Polanyi's ideas about the essential or "core qualities" of effective therapeutic relationships. These qualities include: unconditional positive regard, accurate empathy, and genuineness. The balance of relationship, influence, and responsibility works well to change lives.

It is useful to ask: is developmental change a *significant emotional experience*, or a predictable stage with normative unfolding? Is change an event or a process? This question is useful even though it sounds like an exam question or conundrum. No exam will follow! In therapy's evolution the psychoanalytic approach evolved with the premise that changing personality requires a healing relationship evolving slowly. Transference, interpretation of dreams, defenses, abreaction, working through and the personality changes eventually follow. Freud never had to contend with "managed care," even though he had equally antagonistic nonbelievers. All types of psychotherapy are available, and in recent times there is a cry for empirically supported therapies (translation: prove it works in researched applications). An accepted adage endures that says we must answer the question, "What therapy with what patient under what conditions?"

Change can come from different dimensions. A good model to describe those options comes from Arnold Lazarus's Multimodal approach to comprehensive therapy (1997).

The acronym for his system is BASIC ID. The dimensions include:

Behavior
Affect
Sensations
Imagery
Cognition
Interpersonal issues
Drugs/Biological factors

Lazarus uses these dimensions to conceptualize the strengths and weaknesses, thereby tailoring treatment to the most valuable or preferred angle of approach. We are not aware of a movie about his model, but one can see, touch, smell, and envision the possibilities.

THERAPY (THE BEST OF TIMES, THE WORST OF TIMES)

Movies afford entertaining yet practical examples of: 1) how to use cinema to capture the minimal interference principle in therapy, and 2) how to help clients rewrite life stories that have "gone awry." We consider movie examples of the good, the bad, and the ugly therapy. Editorial opinions are also offered. We may suggest the relative merit or demerit that certain movies demonstrate. Readers can have fun with this idea in your own setting.

William Glasser's reality therapy (1965) emphasizes relationship and commitment. His approach has been effective with a wide range of patients and presentations. One particular group has been adolescent delinquents. Glasser suggests that the relationship between Henry VIII and Thomas More (as shown in the play or the movie) shows the power and leverage of a relationship.

A Man for All Seasons (1966)

This exceptional movie tells the story of one man's haunting influence on another's integrity (or lack thereof). The historical import of the ethical, psychological and even spiritual conflicts are far-reaching on many levels.

The relationship between Thomas More, chancellor of England, and Henry VIII has been suggested by the therapist William Glasser as a model for the relational influence a therapist ought to develop with his clients (with the caveat that the patient shouldn't have to kill the therapist). Rather, the influence was so powerful that it haunted the king. The important dimensions include an honesty about values and the behaviors that follow. Ethical and moral themes abound as King Henry seeks a divorce from his wife, Catherine of Aragon, so he can wed his mistress, Anne Boleyn. This led to events that had Henry break from the pope and declare himself head of the newly created Church of England.

More's influence was so strong that Henry had him killed even though the chancellor did not publicly condemn the act, but only refused to support or consent. The story is replete with moral meaning and relational wisdom. At one point More asked a prosecutor if he would "set aside the law to get at the Devil?" When the courtesan said he would, More questioned, "And when the Devil turned on you, what protection remains?" The film won Academy Award's for best actor, best film, and best screenplay.

We suggest that a therapist can "get his foot in the patient's head." This is an analogy for the influence of integrity, commitment and accountability that develops in effective therapy relationships.

Ordinary People (1980)

A well-acted and powerful story of upper middle-class family's struggle to come to grips with the accidental drowning death of one son, and the suicide attempt by the surviving brother (Timothy Hutton). Mary Tyler Moore is compelling and believable as the cold and rigid mother. Judd Hirsch's portrayal of the therapist is a great model for dealing with adolescents (who are always a challenge). Hirsch develops a relationship without pushing, but also without allowing his reluctant client to hide in self-blame or avoid the healing process. Robert Redford's directing debut is forceful.

Good Will Hunting (1997)

Matt Damon is a young janitor at MIT who happens to be an unsung mathematical genius. A professor discovers the young man and tries to mentor him. It's tough to accomplish until the professor enlists his old friend (Robin Williams) who is a psychotherapist with problems of his own. The task involves having Damon's character overcome his blue-collar background plus his collision with his parole board. William's character's therapy strategies are worth a great deal as food for discussion in training therapists about such things as boundaries, self-disclosure, and when the ends (do or don't) justify the means in treatment. Academy Awards for best actor and best supporting actor.

The Story of Us (1999)

Michelle Pfeiffer, Bruce Willis and even director Rob Reiner cannot elevate this sentimental story of "bickering toward divorce," into any film awards. However, the movie does have a classic scene about therapy that rates "five stars." The couple is in a therapy session arguing, bickering, and struggling with what they want and what they should do. The scene switches to a fantasy stream of consciousness with the couple and both sets of their parents in bed (thankfully clothed). The dialogue that follows this bizarre fantasy is a hilarious cascade of cross-generational projections, guilt's, aspirations and infighting. In 12-step meetings they refer to this as "coulda, shoulda, woulda!" In therapy, projective identification is another way that begins to describe the fun. This scene is superb for training therapists or entertaining good friends for the evening. (The dialogue is already quoted in Chapter 4).

Analyze This (1998)

Robert DeNiro is the anxiety-ridden Don: Paul Vitti. Billy Crystal is the reluctant mob boss's suburban shrink. Lisa Kudrow is Crystal's fiancé, tortured nearly as much and reluctant Crystal. An effective farce that makes hilarious fun of the mobster film genre. DeNiro helped create. Nominated for Golden Globe Awards for best actor and best film-comedy

This movie really works well in psychotherapy class discussions as slapstick hyperbolae to see the broad mistakes. Laughing loosens the budding therapists for a very free dialogue.

Other good films for psychotherapy class discussion:

National Lampoon's: The Don's Analyst (1997)
The Three Faces of Eve (1957)
Agnes of God (1985)
Baton Rouge (1988)

Basic Instinct (1992)

A horrific example of most everything that should not be done as a therapist! The consulting forensic psychology expert working with the detective Michael Douglas is a piece of work (?!). Sharon Stone gave the unforgettable performance on how to distract male authority figures that wish to do you harm.

Tin Cup (1996)

Kevin Costner plays Ron "Tin Cup" McAvoy, a West Texas golf hustler who has the ability, but not the focus, to be on the pro tour. Rene Russo is a psychologist who also happens to be the girlfriend of McAvoy's golf nemesis (Don Johnson). McAvoy gets caught up with the shrink, Russo, seeking her professional skills to help his game and trying to banish "the yips" (ask a golfer if not familiar). He also ends up pursuing Russo's affections as part of the competition with Johnson's character. Richard "Cheech" Marin is McAvoy's caddie and unofficial therapist. Probably Cheech is a more effective therapist than Russo. Just good fun.

A Beautiful Mind (2001)

Russell Crowe delivers a virtuoso performance as the tormented, brilliant mathematician John Forbes Nash. The true story of this man's struggle with psychosis, while winning a Nobel Prize later in his life, is exquisitely acted. Ron Howard's directing is also superb, matching his growing legacy (e.g., *Cocoon*).

Beyond Therapy (1986)

This otherwise average movie is a scathing satire of treatment and shrinks, based on a play by Christopher Durang. It is the story of confused, crazy neurotic couple and their therapists, who are not any saner. Jeff Goldblum, Tom Conti, Glenda Jackson, Julie Hagerty. Something to keep us humble, perhaps?

Captain Newman, MD (1963)

Gregory Peck is the stiff shrink in a VA psych unit in the final months of World War II. Lots of guilt and agonizing, but comic relief is provided by Tony Curtis. Bobby Darin gives a strong performance as the guilt-ridden hero.

Deconstructing Harry (1997)
Author Harry Block writes thinly veiled autobiographical fiction that exposes most everyone he encounters. This includes ex-wives, lovers, friends, and family. This habit seems to aggravate everyone he knows. The premise does make for an interesting effect providing characters and situations with two versions. There is the slant that suits Harry and the other version that is more real than he wants to know or knows how to deal with. Infidelity, divorce, and art are some of the themes. The cast includes Billy Crystal, Elisabeth Shue, Kirstie Alley, Amy Irving, Demi Moore, Richard Benjamin (and more). Who else, but Woody Allen could get all those folks together?

High Anxiety (1977)
Mel Brooks gives one of his trademark products of low brow humor. This time he parodies the Alfred Hitchcock venue. *Psycho*, *Spellbound*, *The Birds*, and *Vertigo* are all properly tweeked and bludgeoned. Madeline Kahn and Harvey Korman help Brooks in this timeless (?) venue.

Beyond Reason (1977)
Body of Influence (1993)
Coming Apart (1969)
Home Movies (1979)
I Don't Buy Kisses Anymore (1992)
I Never Promised You a Rose Garden (1977)
Jade (1995)

Instinct (1999)
Anthony Hopkins is a primatologist who lived with and studied gorillas in the African jungle a little too long. He's been incarcerated and brought back to Miami where the young psychiatrist (Cuba Gooding) has to unravel the conundrum. They spar; they introspect. A kind of *Heart of Darkness* with a side order of the culture of psychiatric residency ambition. Donald Sutherland is the resident's mentor and role model for self-importance but also the Socratic method. The movie is loosely based on Daniel Quinn's book, Ishmael.

Don Juan DeMarco (1995)
Marlon Brando, Johnny Depp, Faye Dunaway.
Brando is a burned-out psychiatrist romantically inspired by a suicidal cape-wearing puzzling man-child (Depp) who thinks he is Don Juan. This "tragic" figure recounts thousands of sexual conquests. The psychiatrist is inspired to spice up his own marriage to Faye Dunaway's character. Depp gives a sincere and engaging performance skirting melodrama. The movie wins no awards for model therapy. However, it is a great piece to start discussion about sexual themes courses on aging or psychotherapy.
Golden Globe Award and Academy Award nominations for best song, *"Have You Ever Really Loved a Woman?"* by Van Morrison.

The Dream Team (1989)
A Fine Madness (1966)

Final Analysis (1992)
Last Rites (1998)
If Lucy Fell (1995)
Mumford (1999)
One Flew Over the Cuckoo's Nest (1975)

The Prince of Tides (1991)
A sprawling southern fried saga of Pat Conroy's novel by the same title. Conroy and his other novels (*The Great Santini, The Water Is Wide, The Lord's of Discipline,* or *Beach Music*) are all fascinating fodder for courses on psychopathology, as well as gripping reading. The dysfunctional Wingo family spreads a pathology from the South to the Big Apple. Barbara Streisand gives a clinic on ethical mistakes psychotherapists can make. The film is worth that alone as a teaching vehicle. Some people's role in life is to serve as a bad example. The movie did get accolades for Nick Nolte. He was an Academy Award nominee for best actor in his role as the patient's brother, and Streisand's complicated diversion.

On a Clear Day You Can See Forever (1970)
The Stranger (1987)
What's New Pussycat? (1965)
Whispers in the Dark (1992)
Wild Country (1971)
Where Truth Lies (1996)
Wild in the Country (1961)

The Young Poisoner's Handbook (1995)
Based on the true story of a London teenager, Graham Young (Hugh O'Conor), is obsessed with chemistry and in conflict with his stepmother. So he poisons her chocolate and her death lands him in the Broadmoor prison for the criminally insane. Dr. Ziegler (Antony Sher) recommends the young man's parole after eight years of treatment. Young then gets a job in a photo lab where he proceeds to poison his co-workers' tea. During his second hospitalization, he writes the handbook. The movie is a lot to swallow, but can be useful in a psychopathology course.

Bad examples are listed by the *Psychotherapy Networker's* annual convention and reported in *Therapy Networker* (June, 2001). A general discussion on how therapists are presented in popular films is worth considering. Some of the best, bad examples of therapists include: the maniacal psychiatrist in *The Cabinet of Dr. Daligari;* the un-sufferable "know it all" in the movie *Psycho*; and the leggy seductive shrink in *Prince of Tides*.

Planning therapy for the couple in *The War of the Roses* (1989) is a great and humbling place to practice marital therapy. "Hell hath no fury like the lawyer of a woman scorned." Michael Douglas, Kathleen Turner and Danny DeVito make an unforgettable trio in love and litigation.

In the area of *group therapy*, the movie *Twelve Angry Men* (1957) is a great practice arena. This movie examines the toughest array of disagreeable jurors imaginable. The trial of a Latino young murder suspect creates an emotionally charged conflict. Henry Fonda's voice of reason in a jury ready to render a quick-and-dirty verdict is compelling. This movie could be used in therapy training to develop understanding and strategies to address resistance and bias. Director Sydney Lumet was nominated for the Academy Award.

Two unrelated irascible men are worth quoting on this theme of conflict:

> If two people agree on everything, one of them is unnecessary.
> —George Bernard Shaw

> If you can't get rid of a family skeleton, you might as well make it dance.
> —George Bernard Shaw

> The lion and the lamb will lie down together, and the lamb won't get much sleep!
> —Woody Allen

Once again (see Chapter 4) we commend the exceptional contributions of the psychiatrist Frank Pittman (1987, 1989, 1993). Pittman writes a regular column "The Screening Room," for the professional periodical *The Family Therapy Networker* (recently renamed *The Therapy Networker: Psychotherapy and Modern Life*). Dr. Pittman's thoughtful, guiding, and provocative style of writing about movies captures the most profound issues in an entertaining way that teaches, cajoles, scolds, and enlightens us. He is a contributing editor for the magazine, which is now available to lay audiences as well. He reviews current cinema and often includes several movies at once to make and clarify the best and worst of solutions and pratfalls in living.

One notable example from his column was a comparison of the lives and works of Marlon Brando, Montgomery Clift, James Dean, and Paul Newman. He considered both their cinematic roles and personal lives in a way that shows the potential and the *shadows* that may cloud the personal growth of such popular figures. Countless other columns guide the way through the morass of psychological pain and emotional health. The depth of his insight is also mined in his books; cited in the attached references.

Another example from Dr. Pittman's 2001 article in the *Networker* was: "Bloodsuckers: The appeal of those who feed on us." He reviewed *Shadow of the Vampire* (John Malkovich, Willem Dafoe); *Hannibal* (Anthony Hopkins's sequel to *Silence of the Lambs*); and Ed Harris and Marcia Gay Harden in *Pollock*. This last film is the story of the famous painter and his mistress/wife who gave up herself for someone who seems stronger and needier.

Pittman points out the strange attraction that individuals or the culture may have to dependent, helpless, tortured sensualists. They cannot communicate outside of their peculiar need, art, or forbidden obsession. These movie examples offer a visceral grasp of the concept of "borderline personalities." They may be the toughest to treat and certainly the toughest to abide.

Therapy Metaphors

Before going directly into movies or popular books about therapy, one movie metaphor that might capture the protracted experience of training (as a therapist), could be the musical *Brigadoon* (1954; Gene Kelly, Van Johnson, Cyd Charisse). This tale is about an eighteenth-century Scottish village that awakens only every 100 years for one day. Two modern day vacationers stumble upon it. The men find the people and the village delightful, and fall in love. The Lerner and Loewe musical score is a classic (e.g., "Heather on the Hill," "Almost Like Being in Love"). Once in the enchanting land they have to make a decision by the end of the day: to stay or leave. If they stay they disappear with the village for another 100 years. But...we digress.

Sheldon Kopp's book, *If You Meet the Buddha on the Road, Kill Him*, and Michael Murphy's article on *The Wizard of Oz*, and the journey of psychotherapy are good source's of discussion about qualities common to all forms of effective therapy.

Sheldon Kopp's historical stories, metaphors, and the tales he uses are sufficiently valuable by themselves. But he also weaves them to describe the journey of therapy in a compelling, humorous and ironic fashion. With the reader he shares: As a child I was so often ...that if I had not found the tales of others in the books I read, I believe I would have died!" (p. 19). The *Epic of Gilgamesh*, the *Garden of Eden, Siddhartha, The Canterbury Tales, Macbeth, Don Quixote*, Dante's *Inferno*, Kafka's ...*The Castle, Pilgrim's Progress*, the *Legend of the Wandering Jew, Heart of Darkness*, excerpts from the *I Ching*; and stories of Kopp's work with memorable patients unfold with wisdom and irony. With movies having been made on most of these classics, his book captures the core dynamics in valuable style.

Kopp also has the valuable gift of laughing at himself. He tells a story about good advice that can backfire. Therapist's kids (of any age) probably hear all kinds of psychobabble. Some is good. Some is probably confusing. Kopp points out that self-determination is a central axiom in much of therapy. With good intentions we preach self-determination to patients (and to) our children. One should not blame situations or other people for our plight or. Circumstance. *"Internal locus of control vs. External locus of control"* (Rotter, 1990) is the fancy name for this theory. Kopp notes how often he hammered this into his son. One day the young man came running through a storm back into the house. Completely soaked as he met his dad in the house, the son said, "Look, I rained all over myself!"

The offspring of psychotherapists may have a special burden to bear, but they often learn the truths better than we imagined.

Kopp's book enjoyed wide popularity when it was written. And we continue to be amazed how often psychotherapy graduate students make reference to its value as they carry along copies (not required reading) of this thoughtful and entertaining book. The archetypal journeys with: paradox self-humor, redemptive change, and new perspective must have some magic yet.

Dorothy and the Journey to OZ

Adapted from L. Frank Baum's children's story. Consider a story and movie that convey the intent, the process and possibilities of psychotherapy. *The Wizard of Oz* has remained in the hearts and minds of several generations. The movie captures puzzles and possibilities of life's journey. Having part of the authors training at the Menninger Clinic and upbringing in the unique state of Kansas, this story may be even more compelling to the author. Dorothy's trip offers an enduring way to think about hopes and fears, demoralization and renewal; and the ability to turn adversity into strength and growth.

Earlier we have drawn from several therapists and writers on the subjects of change, growth and cross-cultural themes. These include Bruno Bettelheim and the message of his book, *The Uses of Enchantment*; Rollo May and his book, *The Courage to Create*, and *The Cry for Myth*; Jerome Frank and his book, *Persuasion and Healing*; Sheldon Kopp's *If You Meet the Buddha on the Road, Kill Him*. Also the contributions of Carl Jung and Joseph Campbell have shaped many venues. G. S. Howard (1991), a social psychologist, has suggested different cultures have their own tales of identity. An individual's identity is an exercise in personal story construction...or telling a life story. Times of difficulty or demoralization are an example of life stories gone awry. And therapy may be thought of as an exercise in story reconstruction.

Viney (1993, as discussed in Chapter 2) offers another variation on that theme in "personal construct" therapy (Kelly, 1955). Viney's approach uses the concepts and terminology of the client rather foisting a new jargon on them. These writers mentioned offer a nexus of qualities that are common to all forms of therapy and change. The good news is that Dorothy makes a lasting application of these concepts. And the movie, as metaphor for growth and understanding; beats any textbook.

Jerome Frank (1991) said that one of the universal qualities of persuasion and healing is an emotionally charged, confiding relationship where there is a prescribed process that creates a change in perspective. This change combats "demoralization" and is hope-engendering and renewing. Martin Seligman (1991) called this acquired outlook "learned optimism."

Dorothy's experience included:

natural disasters (tornado),
powerful impediments and resources (good & bad witches, little people),
group process (farm hands: *aka*: the scarecrow, the tin man and the cowardly lion),
a fine little dog (with energy, curiosity and impulsiveness),
magical slippers, and
a Wizard not clearly good or bad.

Sometimes students and professors have also likened Dorothy's dilemma to graduate school. Ponder that for a moment.

Much of Dorothy's success is related to encouragement rather than to direct confrontation. Her three traveling companions, the lion, tin man, and scarecrow, put aside their worries, which allow them to show qualities they thought they lacked, in order to help Dorothy. Success came from developing and saving what seemed to be weaker parts of themselves rather than simply fighting oppressors or villains. Dorothy becomes a heroine and overcomes the Wicked Witch's forces. Some of that strength also came from caring for her companions.

Finally, Dorothy, and all who share her journey, come to one more realization. When they finally go to see the Wizard and bring the wicked witch's broom (the price of getting their wishes granted), Toto pulls back the curtain and they discover just a man behind the curtain. Dorothy tells the Wizard, "You are a very bad man."

His response is, "I'm really not a bad man. But I'm a very bad wizard!" There is no "powerful other" to make us whole. Dorothy's travels from dependence to independence and then interdependence bring her full circle.

The Wizard attempts to help her return home in the balloon. The impetuous Toto jumps out. Dorothy follows the dog, leaving the Wizard and his ballon. The good witch Glenda reappears and tells Dorothy how to get home on her own (Murphy, 1996).

Her demoralization is replaced by a learned optimism. Competence, intimacy, and courage result. She proclaims that whatever she needs to gain her hearts desire, "is in my own backyard!"

Jerome Frank's (1991) qualities common to all forms of therapy (cited earlier in this chapter) are crucial. The "hope engendering," dimension is both the first and last place to promote healing and growth.

APPENDIX

Case Conceptualization

Presenting Problems

Patient's View
Clinician's View

Developmental Backdrop

Individual
Current Family
Family of Origin

Physical/Medical Related Factors

Life Change & Relevant Stressors

Fun Activities

Core Dynamics
Coping Resources/Limitations

Relational
Cognitive
Affective
Behavioral
Existential

Etiological Core Pattern(s)

Implications For Prognosis & Treatment Strategies

Short-Term & Long-Term Goals
Good Endings

This format for understanding people's core dynamics or personal themes (in several dimensions) may seem daunting at first. However, by practicing its application the dimensions become familiar and offer options for change:

1) First, as a way of considering each area that could be relevant,
2) next, by integrating information in a coherent way. Which gives clues to what "channel" (e.g., the Lazarus' dimensions

of the BASIC ID acronym) or *angle of approach* the client or family prefers; and, consequently
3) we can focus and communicate in the patient's preferred cognitive, emotional or behavioral channel (or language) as an ally!

When the information is gathered (drawing on psychological assessment when possible) we can build on strengths when possible, but also heal losses or trauma as needed.

Add the important practical decisions of:

1) How much can be accomplished in the time allotted?
2) Is this a task of stabilization or change?
3) How can we combat demoralization?
4) Should we foster (for example) a success experience, a mourning experience, or insight?
5) How can we create a good ending to treatment?

The *therapist as a family practitioner* is a helpful analogy. This model includes making interventions at "symptomatic junctures in the life span." This model also allows us to do therapy in episodes rather than a long-term process. Long-term therapy is rarer in this age of managed care. The patient's *history of endings* becomes even more relevant when we must do therapy in a limited time frame or in periodic episodes of therapy across the life span. A good ending has benefit for losses in the past and hope for the future. Begin with the end in mind!

Colleagues and students who use this model generally appreciate the balance of practicality with a thorough understanding of the potential contributions from patients' hopes, fears, and history. As one sage put it, "What the patient needs is a good listening to!"

REFERENCES

Archer, R. P. and Peake, T. H. (1984). Learning and teaching psychotherapy. In Peake, T. H. & Archer, R. P. (eds). *Clinical training in psychotherapy.* New York: Haworth Press.

Doehrman, M. J. (1976). Parallel process in supervision of psychotherapy. *Bulletin of the Menninger Clinic. 40*, 71–84.

Friedman, D. and Kaslow, N. (1986). The development of professional identity in psychotherapists: Six stages in the supervision process. *The Clinical Supervisor, 4,* 29–50.

Frank, J. D. and Frank, J. B. (1991). *Persuasion and healing: A comparative study of psychotherapy.* Baltimore: Johns Hopkins University Press.

Fromm, Erika (1976). Altered states of consciousness and ego psychology. *Social Science Review, 50,* 557–569.

Fromm, Erika (1981). Primary and secondary process in waking and in altered states of consciousness. *Academic Psychology Bulletin, 3*, 29–45.

Gabbard, G.O. (2001). *Psychoanalysis and film.* New York: Karnac.

Glasser, William (1965). *Reality therapy: A new approach to psychiatry.* New York: Harper & Row.

Hess, A. K. (1980). *Psychotherapy supervision.* New York: Wiley

Howard, G. S. (1991). Culture tales: A narrative approach to thinking, cross-cultural psychology, and psychotherapy. *American Psychologist, 46,* 187–197.

Jung, C. (1984). *Dream analysis.* Princeton, NJ: Princeton University Press.

Kelly, George (1955). *The psychology of personal constructs.* New York: Norton.

Kopp, Sheldon (1972). *If You meet the Buddha on the road, kill him: The pilgrimage of psychotherapy patients.* Ben Lomond, CA: Science and Behavior Books.

Lazarus, Arnold A. (1997). *Brief but comprehensive psychotherapy: The multimodal way.* New York: Springer.

Mowrer, Hobart (Ed.) (1953). *Psychotherapy: Theory and research.* New York: McGraw-Hill.

Murphy, Michael S. (1996). The Wizard of OZ as a cultural narrative and conceptual model for psychotherapy. *Psychotherapy: Theory, research, practice and training, 4,* 531–538.

Pittman, Frank (1987). *Turning points: Treatment of families in transition and crisis.* New York: Norton.

Pittman, Frank (1989). *Private lies: Infidelity and the betrayal of intimacy.* New York: Norton.

Pittman, Frank (1993). *Man enough: Fathers, sons, and the search for masculinity.* New York: Perigee Books.

Polanyi, Michael (1966). *The tacit dimension.* New York: Doubleday/Anchor.

Ralph, N. B. (1980). Learning psychotherapy: A developmental perspective. *Psychiatry, 43,* 243–250.

Rotter, J. B. (1975). Some problems and misconceptions related to the construct of internal versus external control of reinforcement. *Journal of Consulting and Clinical Psychology. 43,* 56–67.

Rotter, J. B. (1990). Internal versus external control of reinforcement: A case history of a variable. *American Psychologist, 45,* 489–493.

Satir, Virginia (1988). *The new peoplemaking.* Mountain View, CA: Science and Behavior Books.

Seligman, Martin (1991). *Learned optimism.* New York: Knopf.

Martin Seligman, at the University of Pennsylvania, used his time while president of the American Psychological Association as a "bully pulpit," to explain and promote *learned optimism* or positive psychology. He recently raised $20 million to support his efforts to develop a classification system for identifying positive traits such as creativity, curiosity and fairness. He has an online questionnaire to help the reader gauge their resources.

www.psych.upenn.edu/seligman/strengths.

Van de Castle, R. L. (1994). *Our dreaming mind.* New York: Ballantine
Viorst, Judith (1986). *Necessary losses.* New York: Simon & Schuster.
Wedding, D. and Boyd, M. (1999). *Movies and mental illness: Using films to understand psychopathology.* New York: McGraw-Hill College.

8
Diversions, Fascinations, and Awards

Too many good movies to be recalled.
Too many bad movies to be remembered.
This potpourri of eras, images and themes is more like popcorn than a real meal. However the focus is on entertainment more than scholarly focus.

Modern Maturity magazine (American Association of Retired People) offers their list of "Best Movies for Grown-ups." Their award is called The Golden Chair (*Las Chaise D'Or*) Some of their recent picks (2001) include: *Lantana* which is a moral fable in which betrayal has consequences, integrity is rewarded and that every day decisions can bedevil us at any age.

Some other recent award winners in 2001 included:
Under the Sand (best foreign film) with a theme of reaching an age where you realize life's most nagging questions might never be answered.

Shrek won as the best movie for *Grown-Ups who refuse to grow up*. Tom Wilkinson was named best actor for *In the Bedroom*, and Robert Altman for *Gosford Park*.

Another entertaining angle on movies is the approach taken by *TV Guide* (March 24–30, 2001). They submitted their list of the: "50 Greatest Movie Moments" (not to be confused with the greatest movies).

    50   *Goldfinger* ('64) gadgets.
           Heat ('95) Pacino and DeNiro—what a duel!
           Matrix ('99) freeze-frame and alien threat.
           When Harry Met Sally ('89) Men and Women and Meg Ryan-Faking It.
           Dr. Strangelove ('63) The Cold War and Slim Pickens riding the bomb.

45   *Big* ('88) Tom Hanks—dancing on the big piano
     Star Wars ('77) the Cantina of aliens.
     Something About Mary ('98) Cameron Diaz—hair gel—the seed is flung.
     Dirty Harry ('71) Clint Eastwood— do I feel lucky?
     Alien (' 79) gut buster—parasite emerges.

40   *High Noon* ('52) Gary Cooper—shoot out (a political parable).
     Saturday Night Fever ('77) disco till you drop (or heave).
     The Deer Hunter ('78) C Walken, R. DeNiro—Russian roulette.
     The Graduate ('67) D. Hoffman, Mrs. Robinson's hosiery.
     Public Enemy ('31) James Cagney—"Top of the World, Ma!"

35   *Five Easy Pieces* ('70) Jack Nicholson's oddly troubled character who frightens the waitress in a roadside diner telling her to "hold the chicken between your legs!" as he violently clears the tabletop.
     All About Eve ('50) Bette Davis "fasten your seatbelts, it's gonna be a bumpy night."
     Glory ('89) Denzel Washington—the single tear after the flogging.
     Cabaret ('72) Bob Fosse's stylized view of cabaret and Hitler youth.
     The Birds ('63) Tippi Hedren terror of malevolent crows.

30   *Annie Hall* ('77) Diane Keaton many favorite scenes, but "running subtitles" of stream of consciousness during flirtation.
     Lady and the Tramp ('55) The child in all of us.
     Sunset Boulevard ('50) Gloria Swanson and DeMille's fleeting fame & descent into lunacy.
     From Here to Eternity ('53) B. Lancaster and D. Kerr—the lip-lock, the surf and the beach.
     The Phantom of the Opera ('25) Lon Chaney the phantom unmasked.

25   *Network* ('76) Peter Finch the outraged anchorman, "I'm mad as hell and I'm not going to take it anymore!"

Diversions, Fascinations, and Awards 115

Goodfellas ('90) Joe Pesci, Ray Liotta the terrifying speech, "Funny how? I amuse you!?"
Chinatown ('74) Jack Nicholson John Huston in Roman Polanski's greed and incest in Los Angeles.
Citizen Kane ('41) Orson Welles and a new level of movie sophistication.
2001: A Space Odyssey ('68) Kubrick's dismantling the calculating computer HAL 9000.

20 *North by Northwest* ('59) Alfred Hitchcock convinces Cary Grant and the world...you're not safe anywhere.
Jaws ('75) The primordial and archetypal monster, the old salt, the young professor and delicious terror.
The Exorcist ('73) More terror, good and evil, Linda Blair and a swiveling head from William Friedkin.
Battleship Potemkin ('25) Silent screen masterpiece of 1905 Russian revolutionary uprising and Czarist troops massacre leaving an empty baby carriage bouncing down stairs Sergei Eisenstein.
To Kill a Mockingbird ('62) Gregory Peck (Atticus), Robert Duvall (Boo) and an archetype of good and evil.

15 *The Seven Year Itch* ('55) Billy Wilder's exposure of Marylin Monroe's white dress billowing over the subway grate. Was there a plot as well?
It's a Wonderful Life ('46) Jimmy Stewart and Frank Capra's enduring holiday gift of hope and sentimentality.
On the Waterfront ('54) Elia Kazan's classic of broken boxer fighting corruption and regret. Rod Steiger and Marlon Brando: "I coulda had class. I coulda been a contender."
Bonnie and Clyde ('67) Arthur Penn's controversial foray into violence and the Depression—era notorious outlaws. Did he blow away his antiheroes (Faye Dunaway and Warren Beatty) along with the lure of criminal life?
Taxi Driver ('76) Mirror Image. Not the last of the "crazed Vietnam Veteran" genre, but an unforgettable portrayal. Martin Scorcese's study of the Robert DeNiro loner. Jodie Foster's debut, and a story written by the reluctant Calvinist, Paul Schrader.

10   *Titanic* ('97) The splashiest moment in the greatest disaster movie in recollection. A griping metaphor with mythic proportions and implications. James Cameron's $200 million tribute to high tech.

A Night at the Opera ('35). The Stateroom and the Marx Brothers inspired insanity, stream of consciousness and unrivaled humor thumbing the nose at everything possible.

Singin' in the Rain ('52) The rain dance to remember. Gene Kelly and Debbie Reynolds.

The Wizard of OZ ('39) The baby boomers' mythic classic adapted from L. Frank Baum's children's story. Judy Garland's Dorothy, her traveling companions, and the wizard who's "not a bad man, just a bad wizard," continue to enchant and inspire.

Gone With the Wind ('39) 1939 was a memorable year for cinema. Margaret Mitchell's bestseller and Scarlet as an archetype who could only be matched by Rhett Butler. A romanticizing of the civil war that still haunts us.

5   *Psycho* ('60) Alfred Hitchcock's genius for terror and Bernard Herrmann's brilliant score "fill up our senses," with previously unknown terror about showers, motels and wigs.

King Kong ('33) The greatest monster movie of its day continues to set a standard. Erotically monumental symbolism and innovative in animation and special effects.

The Godfather ('72) An offer he can't refuse and the horse's mane scene. Francis Ford Coppola shows a savage world that eerily fascinates.

Casablanca ('72) Bogart and Bergman and the foggy airfield. "Our problems don't amount to a hill of beans" as the romantic sacrifice.

Saving Private Ryan ('98) The most realistic and wrenching combat movie ever made. Steven Spielberg resurrects the terror, chaos, and eventually the sacrificing heroism of a generation.

AWARDS

One way to show eras or generations through movies is to sample those that have been set apart for message, quality, creativity, social import or emotional honesty. These awards may be a resource to explore shared changes of fashion, values, hopes and fears, and historical themes across the decades.

Diversions, Fascinations, and Awards   117

American Film Institute's Best of 100 Years
1. *Citizen Kane* (1941)
2. *Casablanca* (1942)
3. *The Godfather* (1972)
4. *Gone With the Wind* (1939)
5. *Lawrence of Arabia* (1962)
6. *The Wizard of Oz* (1939)
7. *The Graduate* (1967)
8. *On the Waterfront* (1954)
9. *Schindler's List* (1993)
10. *Singin' in the Rain* (1952)
11. *It's a Wonderful Life* (1946)
12. *Sunset Boulevard* (1950)
13. *The Bridge on the River Kwai* (1957)
14. *Some Like It Hot* (1959)
15. *Star Wars* (1977)
16. *All About Eve* (1950)
17. *The African Queen* (1951)
18. *Psycho* (1960)
19. *Chinatown* (1974)
20. *One Flew Over the Cuckoo's Nest* (1975)
21. *The Grapes of Wrath* (1940)
22. *2001: A Space Odyssey* (1968)
23. *The Maltese Falcon* (1941)
24. *Raging Bull* (1980)
25. *E.T. the Extra-Terrestrial* (1982)
26. *Dr. Strangelove* (1964)
27. *Bonnie and Clyde* (1967)
28. *Apocalypse Now* (1979)
29. *Mr. Smith Goes to Washington* (1939)
30. *Treasure of the Sierra Madre* (1948)
31. *Annie Hall* (1977)
32. *The Godfather Part II* (1974)
33. *High Noon* (1952)
34. *To Kill a Mockingbird* (1962)
35. *It Happened One Night* (1934)
36. *Midnight Cowboy* (1969)
37. *The Best Years of Our Lives* (1946)
38. *Double Indemnity* (1944)
39. *Doctor Zhivago* (1965)
40. *North by Northwest* (1959)
41. *West Side Story* (1961)
42. *Rear Window* (1954)
43. *King Kong* (1933)
44. *The Birth of a Nation* (1915)
45. *A Streetcar Named Desire* (1951)
46. *A Clockwork Orange* (1971)

American Film Institute's 100 Passions—100 Best Love Stories
Casablanca (1942)
Gone With the Wind (1939)
West Side Story (1961)
Roman Holiday (1953)
An Affair to Remember (1957)
The Way We Were (1973)
Doctor Zhivago (1965)
It's a Wonderful Life (1946)
Love Story (1970)
City Lights (1931)
Annie Hall (1977)
My Fair Lady (1964)
Out of Africa (1985)

The African Queen (1951)
Wuthering Heights (1939)
Singin' in the Rain (1952)
Moonstruck (1987)
Vertigo (1958)
Ghost (1990)
From Here to Eternity (1953)

Pretty Woman (1990)
On Golden Pond (1981)
Now, Voyager (1942)
King Kong (1933)
When Harry Met Sally (1989)
The Lady Eve (1941)
The Sound of Music (1965)
The Shop Around the Corner (1940)
An Officer and a Gentleman (1982)

Swing Time (1936)

The King and I (1956)
Dark Victory (1939)
Camille (1937)
Beauty and the Beast (1991)
Gigi (1958)
Random Harvest (1942)
Titanic (1997)

It Happened One Night (1934)
An American in Paris (1951)
Nonotchka (1939)
Funny Girl (1968)
Anna Karenina (1935)
A Star Is Born (1954)
The Philadelphia Story (1940)
Sleepless in Seattle (1993)
To Catch a Thief (1955)

118 Cinema and Life Development

47. *Taxi Driver* (1976)
48. *Jaws* (1975)
49. *Snow White and the Seven Dwarfs* (1937)
50. *Butch Cassidy and the Sundance Kid* (1969)
51. *The Philadelphia Story* (1940)
52. *From Here to Eternity* (1953)
53. *Amadeus* (1984)
54. *All Quiet on the Western Front* (1930
55. *The Sound of Music* (1965)
56. *M*A*S*H* (1970)
57. *The Third Man* (1949)
58. *Fantasia* (1940)
59. *Rebel Without a Cause* (1955)
60. *Raiders of the Lost Ark* (1981)
61. *Vertigo* (1958)
62. *Tootsie* (1982)
63. *Stagecoach* (1939)
64. *Close Encounters of the Third Kind* (1977)
65. *The Silence of the Lambs* (1991)
66. *Network* (1976)
67. *The Manchurian Candidate* (1962)
68. *An American in Paris* (1951)
69. *Shane* (1953)
70. *The French Connection* (1971)
71. *Forrest Gump* (1994)
72. *Ben-Hur* (1959)
73, *Wuthering Heights* (1939)
74. *The Gold Rush* (1925)
75. *Dances with Wolves* (1990)
76. *City Lights* (1931)
77. *American Graffiti* (1973)
78. *Rocky* (1976)
79. *The Deer Hunter* (1978)
80. *The Wild Bunch* (1969)
81. *Modern Times* (1936)
82. *Giant* (1956)
83. *Platoon* (1986)
84. *Fargo* (1996)
85. *Duck Soup* (1933)
86. *Mutiny on the Bounty* (1935)
87. *Frankenstein* (1931)
88. *Easy Rider* (1969)
89. *Patton* (1970)
90. *The Jazz Singer* (1927)
91. *My Fair Lady* (1964)
92. *A Place in the Sun* (1951)
93. *The Apartment* (1960)
94. *Goodfellas* (1990)

Splendor in the Grass (1961)
Last Tango in Paris (1972)
The Postman Always Rings Twice (1946)
Shakespeare in Love (1998)

Bringing Up Baby (1938)
The Graduate (1967)
A Place in the Sun (1951)
Sabrina (1954)

Reds (1981)
The English Patient (1996)
Two for the Road (1967)
Guess Who's Coming to Dinner (1967)
Picnic (1955)
To Have and Have Not (1944)
Breakfast at Tiffany's (1961)
The Apartment (1960)
Sunrise (1927)
Marty (1955)

Bonnie and Clyde (1967)
Manhattan (1979)
A Streetcar Named Desire (1951)

What's Up, Doc? (1972)
Harold and Maude (1971)
Sense and Sensibility (1995)
Way Down East (1920)
Roxanne (1987)
The Ghost and Mrs. Muir (1947)
Woman of the Year (1942)
The American President (1995)
The Quiet Man (1952)
The Awful Truth (1937)
Coming Home (1978)
Jezebel (1939)
The Sheik (1921)
The Goodbye Girl (1977)
Witness (1985)
Morocco (1930)
Double Indemnity (1944)
Love is a Many-Splendored Thing (1955)
Notorious (1946)
The Unbearable Lightness of Being (1988)
The Princess Bride (1987)
Who's Afraid of Virginia Woolf? (1966)
The Bridges of Madison County (1955)
Working Girl (1988)
Porgy and Bess (1959)
Dirty Dancing (1987)
Body Heat (1981)

Diversions, Fascinations, and Awards   119

95. *Pulp Fiction* (1994)
96. *The Searchers* (1956)
97. *Bringing Up Baby* (1938)
98. *Unforgiven* (1992)
99. *Guess Who's Coming to Dinner* (1967)
100. *Yankee Doodle Dandy* (1942)

Lady and the Tramp (1955)
Barefoot in the Park (1967)
Grease (1978)
The Hunchback of Notre Dame (1939)
Pillow Talk (1959)

Jerry Maguire (1996)

American Academy Awards	**1920s**	**British Academy Awards**

Wings
Broadway Melody

1930s

All Quiet on the Western Front
Cimarron
Grand Hotel
Cavalcade
It Happened One Night
Mutiny on the Bounty
The Great Ziegfield
The Life of Emile Zola
You Can't Take It with You
Gone With the Wind

1940s

Rebecca
How Green Was My Valley
Mrs. Miniver
Casablanca
Going My Way
The Lost Weekend
The Best Years of Our Lives
Gentleman's Agreement
Hamlet
All the King's Men

The Best Years of Our Lives
Odd Man Out
The Fallen Idol
Hamlet
The Bicycle Thief
The Third Man

1950s

All About Eve
An American in Paris
The Greatest Show on Earth
From Here to Eternity
On the Waterfront
Marty
Around the World in 80 Days
The Bridge on the River Kwai
Gigi
Ben-Hur

All About Eve
The Blue Lamp
La Ronde
The Lavender Hill Mob
Forbidden Games
Genevieve
Hobson's Choice
Wages of Fear
Richard III
Gervaise
Reach for the Sky
The Bridge on the Rive Kwai
Room at the Top
Ben-Hur
Sapphire

120 Cinema and Life Development

1960s

The Apartment	*The Apartment*
West Side Story	*Saturday Night and Sunday Morning*
Lawrence of Arabia	*The Hustler*
Tom Jones	*A Taste of Honey*
My Fair Lady	*Lawrence of Arabia*
The Sound of Music	*Tom Jones*
A Man for All Seasons	*Dr. Strangelove*
In the Heat of the Night	*The Icress File*
Oliver	*My Fair Lady*
Midnight Cowboy	*The Spy Who Came in from the Cold*
	Who's Afraid of Virginia Woolf?
	A Man for All Seasons
	The Graduate
	Midnight Cowboy

1970s

Patton	*Butch Cassidy and the Sundance Kit*
The French Connection	*Sunday, Bloody Sunday*
The Godfather	*Cabaret*
The Sting	*Day for Night*
The Godfather, Part 2	*Alice Doesn't Live Here Anymore*
One Flew Over the Cuckoo's Nest	*One Flew Over the Cuckoo's Nest*
Rocky	*Annie Hall*
Annie Hall	*Julie*
The Deer Hunter	*Manhattan*
Kramer versus Kramer	

1980s

Ordinary People	*The Elephant Man*
Chariots of Fire	*Chariots of Fire*
Ghandi	*Ghandi*
Terms of Endearment	*Educating Rita*
Amadeus	*The Killing Fields*
Out of Africa	*The Purple Rose of Cairo*
Platoon	*A Room with a View*
The Last Emperor	*Hope and Glory*
Rain Man	*Jean de Florette*
Driving Miss Daisy	*The Last Emperor*
	Dead Poets Society

1990s

Dances with Wolves	*Goodfellas*
The Silence of the Lambs	*The Committments*

Diversions, Fascinations, and Awards 121

Unforgiven *Unforgiven*
Schlinder's List *Schindler's List*
Forrest Gump *Shadowlands*
Braveheart *Four Weddings and a*
 Funeral
The English Patient *Sense and Sensibility*
Titanic *The English Patient*
Shakespeare in Love *The Full Monty*
American Beauty *Nil by Mouth*
 Elizabeth
 Shakespeare in Love
 American Beauty
 East Is East

2000s

Gladiator
A Beautiful Mind
Chicago

Select Bibliography

This list is more a catalog than a narrative. Included are some general references and some web sites (which likely proliferate regularly), plus valuable other resources to get to OZ, or to "get back to Kansas," as Dorothy might say.

GENERAL SOURCES

Carlsen, Mary Baird (1991). *Creative aging: A meaning making perspective.* New York: Norton.
Hornstein, Percy (ed.) (1973). *Reader's companion to world literature.* New York: Mentor-Penguin Books.
Journal of Narrative and Life History. Hillsdale, NJ: Lawrence Erlbaum Associates
Pitman, Frank. The Screening Room. Regular column for *The Therapy Networker.* (formerly *Family Therapy Networker*) (http://psychotherapynetworker.com)

Books

Bertoluccus: The last emperor: Multiple takes (1985). Edited by Bruce Sklarew (Baltimore-Washington Psychoanalytic Society), Bonnie Kaufman (Clinical Professor of Psychiatry-Columbia University), Ellen Handler Spitz (Author of Art and Psyche. Yale University Press (1985) and Diane Borden-faculty San Francisco Psychoanalytic Society and Chair of Film Program. University of Pacific.
Cinematherapy: The Girl's Guide to Movies for Every Mood (1999). Nancy Peske and Beverly West. New York: Dell.
The directors. Robert Emery (1999). Thirteen Directors in their own words. Los Angeles: TV Books.

Great scenes and monologues for actors (1998). Michael Schulman and Eva Mekler. New York: St. Martin's Paperbacks.

The motion picture prescription (1995) Gary Solomon. Santa Rosa, CA: Aslon.

Our dreaming mind. (1994). New York: Ballantine.

Pretty in pink: The golden age of TV teenage movies. (1997). New York: St. Martins Griffin.

Psychoanalysis and film (2001). Glen Gabbard (ed.) New York: Karnac. Includes: *Wild Strawberries, Vertigo, The Crying Game, The Conformist, Reservoir Dogs, Night Moves, Lone Star, Il Postino, Truffaut, The Piano, Crumb, The English Patient, The Remains of the Day, Dirty Harry, Titanic, Deep Impact, Chinatown, Saving Private. Ryan, M* (1931), *Eve's Bayou, Peeping Tom, Erotica, Boys Don't Cry,* and *Being John Malkovich*

Psycho paths: Tracking the serial killer through contemporary american film and fiction. (2000). Phillip Simpson. Carbondale: Southern Illinois Press. Samples various movies (e.g., *Kiss the Girls, Seven, Natural Born Killers, American Psycho, Silence of the Lambs*). The extreme!

Rent 2 films and let's talk in the morning (1998). J. Hesley and G. Hesley. New York: Wiley.

TLA film and video guide: The discerning film lover's guide (2001). Bleir, D. (genre's, themes, country of origin of films). New York: St. Martin's Press.

Treasures of the silver screen (2000). Gynnath Ford. Nashville: Highlands Publishers.

Variety movie guide (2001). 9th ed. Editors of *Variety*. New York: Perigree Books.

Video hounds: The golden retriever: Movies on video and ways to track them down (2001, 2002). New York: Visible Ink.

Wedding, D. and Boyd, M. (1999). *Movies and mental illness: Using films to understand psychopathology.* New York: McGraw-Hill. This resource includes an appendix with a 70-page list of films illustrating psychopathology with diagnostic categories to accompany the DSM-IV.

Woody Allen on Woody Allen (in conversation with Stig Bjorkman). (1993). New York: Grove Press.

The writer's journey 2nd ed. Mythic structure for writers (1998). Studio City, CA: Christopher Vogler. Michael Wiese Productions.

Web sites

http://allmovie.com
http://aging.ufl.edu/apa div20/cinema.htm
http://us.imdb.com
http://movies@oxygen.com
http://turnerclassicmovies

American Film Institute (afionline.org)
American Movie Classics (amctv.com)

FILM 100 (film100.com)
The Greatest Films; (filmsite.org)
The Mining Co. (classic film.miningco.com
UCLA Film/TV Archive (cinema.ucla.edu)
History of film & background on studios & directors
Errors in movies (movie-mistakes.com)
Women; (ivanhoe.com/smartwoman) then click "taketwomovies" link

"Google" is a good launching pad for movie information.

Other Web Sites

(They come and go) with brief descriptions. Some can be opened through windows media, others require Quick Time or Real Video. Obviously, a sound card would be beneficial.

Quicktime - http://www.apple.com/trailers/ Apple's official Quicktime Movie Trailer page with the newest and preview release trailers.
Movies.com - http://movies.go.com/trailers/index.html. Upcoming movie news and trailers.
Hollywood.com http://www.hollywood.com/stories/multimedia/trailers.html View the latest movie trailers and also access a fully searchable movie previews database.
Trailervision - http://www.trailervision.com. Satirical trailers of movies that don't exist.
First Look - http://www.firstlook.com/intheaters. All the latest trailers with release dates, plot synopsis, cast information, links to official sites and member reviews.
The Trailer Park - http://www.movie-trailers.com/. Online guide to movie previews, video clips, film and multimedia from upcoming, current, and classic films.
ZENtertainment - http://zentertainment.com/. Large, weekly-updated collection of links to film preview downloads.
Ad Critic - http://www.adcritic.com/trailers/. Features latest movie trailers with a small archive of less recent releases.
Countingdown Theater - http://www.countingdown.com/theater/. Watch independent and major movie trailers as well as original
programming.
Cinema Confidential: Upcoming Movies-http://www.cinecon.com/trailers.html. Links to trailers for upcoming movies.
Jurassic Punk - http://www.jurassicpunk.com. The oldest and one of the largest movie trailer sites online. Regularly updated.
JoBlo's Movie Trailers - http://www.joblo.com/movietrailers.htm. Great source of movie trailers and teasers.
Dark Horizons - http://www.darkhorizons.com/trailers/. The Ultimate Movie Clips - http://www.ultimatemovieclips.com/pages/index_2.shtml.
Extensive listing of movie clips and trailers.

Fan-Made - http://www.fanmadetrailers.com. Movie previews and trailers edited and chosen by fans.

My Movies - http://www.mymovies.net/include/site/nav_pages/trailers.asp. New release movie trailers.

Movie-Page - http://www.movie-page.com/trailers.htm. Huge trailer archive. Updated regularly.

Hot Trailers - http://hottrailers.com. Movie news, rumors, reviews, releases, and trailers.

Blackjack Films -American Dreamer http://www.blackjackfilms.com/video.htm. Trailer for the independent documentary film American Dreamer.

Pete's Movie Page -http://www.petesmoviepage.com/trailers.shtml. Trailers old and new.

Clipland - http://www.clipland.com/index_mtd.shtml. Large database of movie trailers past and present.

Lights Out Entertainment -http://lightsoutentertainment.com/html/films.shtml. Trailers for Lights Out Entertainment productions.

Film Tease - http://www.filmtease.com. Free flowing reviews on movie trailers with accompanying links to the
trailer.

ScreenDragon - http://www.screendragon.com. Play the latest movie trailers as high-quality, full-screen video screensavers.

Internet Movies - http://www.internetmovies.com.

Hollywood Stars and Eyes
http://www.hollywoodstarsandeyes.com/movies/downloads.htm. Links to newer movie trailers and teasers.

Empire Movies - http://www.empiremovies.com/trailers.shtml.
Links to past and present trailers with short synopsis of each film included.

FilmZone - http://www.filmzone.com/trailers.htm. Links to trailers past and present.

Vidbot - http://www.vidbot.com/cgi/Find?Sect=trail. Over 375 movie trailers, new and old, and counting.

Matt's Music Page - http://www.mattsmusicpage.com/videos.htm. Movie trailers and music videos.

Go Movie Trailers - http://www.gomovietrailers.com. The newest movie downloads, movie listings and movie clips as well as
tickets.

Killer Movies - http://killermovies.com/trailers/. Features links to classic and the newest/preview release trailers.

Movie-Trailers - http://movie-trailers.virtualave.net/ab.html. Links to movie trailers new and old.

4w-movies.com - http://4w-movies.com/trailers/. Links to current release trailers.

Always on TV - http://www.alwaysontv.com/trailers.htm. Movie trailers, streaming video, television shows and personal video.

Slipstream - http://www.slipstreamentertainment.com/movietrailerstitle.htm.
Links to new and old movie trailers.

FilmWorld - http://www.filmworld.co.uk/trailers.htm. View trailers and shorts of most of the new released films provided by Film.com.

Trailer Talk - http://trailertalk.50megs.com. In depth commentary on new and old movie trailers featuring photos, cast information, plot details, and release dates.

Sci-Fi Movies - http://www.geocities.com/giorgos333/index.html. Here you can find trailers, news and interesting facts about science fiction movies.

STP2001 Movie Page -http://www.skunkpro.com/stp2001/news/moviepre.html. Links to recent movie trailers.

Moondog's Reel Audio - http://members.nbci.com/reelaudio/. A one of a kind archive featuring radio commercials of classic and
contemporary films in Real Audio.

Lycos TV - http://tv.lycos.com/cgi-bin/startse.pl?Mo. Movie trailers from all the major studios. Trailers include action,
comedy, drama and family along with trailers of movies currently in video stores and movies coming soon to the theatres.

Trailers World - http://www.trailersworld.com. Movie trailers and information about upcoming releases.

Entertainment Weekly rates the latest movie.trailers www.ew.com/ew/report/0,6115,169044~1~0~ewrateslatestmovie,00.

Subject Index

Abreaction, 80, 99
Academy Awards, 38, 45, 62, 69, 101
   American, 119
   British, 119
Adolescence, 16, 18, 25, 30, 88, 90
Adolescents, 52, 73, 90, 101
Advantages, 53, 98
Affairs, 6
Age cohorts, 90
Aging, 8, 9, 25, 39, 41, 53, 54, 67, 71, 103, 123, 124
Alienation, 6, 72
Allen, Woody, 18, 22, 26, 73, 77, 103, 105, 124
Altman, Robert, 45, 62, 88, 91, 113
An Irish Prayer, 63
Analogy, 2, 4, 35, 98, 101, 110
Anger, 1, 9, 27, 31, 60, 66, 67, 74, 76
Angst, 44, 67, 71, 88
Anonymous, 46, 50, 77, 95
Anxieties, 7, 25
Anxiety, 86, 101, 103
Anxiety-ridden, 101
Appreciation, 2, 6, 31, 37, 43, 53, 58

Approach, 38, 41, 58, 94, 95, 98, 100, 107, 110, 111, 113
   collaborative, 98
   multimodal, 100
   psychoanalytic, 99
Archetypal value, 4, 94
Archetypes, 2, 53, 87, 90
Assault, 49
Assumptive world, 51
At risk, 81, 82
Attitudes, 4, 77
Autonomic nervous system, 81, 82
   parasympathetic, 81
   sympathetic, 46, 81
Autonomy, 11, 15, 22
Award(s), 2, 14, 18, 28, 37, 38, 45, 48, 49, 50, 53, 58, 59, 60, 61, 62, 63, 65, 67, 72, 90, 101, 102, 103, 104, 105, 113, 116

Baby boomers, 90, 116
Bad examples (movies), 44, 104
Bad habits, 2
Basic Id, 100, 110
Behavior(s), 7, 25, 41, 51, 54, 75, 95, 98, 99, 100, 111
Beliefs, 7, 13, 47, 98
Benefits, 1, 36, 43

Subject Index

Bettelheim, Bruno, 2, 4, 5, 30, 107
Books, 7, 8, 9, 29, 31, 32, 33, 36, 39, 41, 55, 57, 59, 66, 67, 74, 83, 84, 85, 89, 91, 95, 105, 106, 111, 123, 124
Borderline personality(ies), 53, 99, 105
Boundaries, 21, 101
Brando, Marlon, 71, 72, 103, 105, 115
Bridge, 80, 84, 85, 117, 119
    emotional, 80
Brokaw, Tom, 85, 89, 91
Burns, George, 28
Burns, Robert, 2
Byrne, Robert, 1

Caplan, Gerald, 80
Case conceptualization, 13, 39
Catharsis, 77, 80
Cather, Willa, 2, 30
Cause,
    & effect, 72
Challenges, 1, 2, 11, 12, 13, 34, 47, 57, 61, 73, 85, 86, 90, 93, 94, 98
Change(s), 4, 5, 6, 7, 11, 12, 13, 21, 33, 35, 37, 39, 41, 50, 53, 61, 64, 71, 81, 83, 96, 97, 98, 99, 100, 106, 107, 109, 110
    developmental, 9, 99
    life, 1, 2, 3, 4, 5, 8, 9, 11, 12, 13, 14, 17, 18, 19, 20, 21, 22, 26, 31, 34, 35, 37, 39, 41, 43, 44, 45, 47, 48, 49, 51, 54, 57, 58, 59, 61, 62, 64, 65, 67, 68, 70, 71, 73, 74, 80, 81, 83, 86, 89, 90, 91, 93, 94, 96, 98, 99, 100, 102, 104, 107, 110, 113, 115
Chocolat, 50
Cinema, 1, 2, 3, 8, 12, 33, 34, 35, 36, 37, 38, 39, 40, 44, 45, 52, 58, 66, 77, 78, 83, 85, 88, 96, 97, 98, 100, 105, 116
    lustful, 77
Cinematherapy, 7, 9, 26, 32, 64, 74, 123
Client-centered therapy, 99

Clift, Montgomery, 71, 72, 105
Cohort, 33, 89
Comedy(ies), 2, 14, 18, 22, 26, 45, 52, 58, 61, 62, 65, 77, 82, 86, 87, 89, 96, 102, 127
Commitment, 3, 4, 7, 21, 70, 98, 100, 101
Communication theory, 7
Compassion, 45, 50
Complementary processes,
    assimilation and accommodation, 3
    form and passion, 38
    stabilization and change, 3
Components, 2, 54, 97
Concept(s), 1, 3, 6, 12, 15, 36, 44, 46, 47, 77, 80, 84, 85, 90, 94, 95, 99, 105, 107
    loss, 3, 85
    of creativity, 3
    sociological, 60, 85
Conceptualization, 13, 39, 109
Conclusions, 97
Conflict, 1, 6, 15, 27, 52, 104, 105
Conscious, 7, 38, 97, 98
Consequences, 113
Control, 7, 35, 70, 82, 106, 111
Conundrum, 1, 99, 103
Core dynamics, 12, 31, 35, 97, 98, 106, 109
Core patterns, 34
Cornerstones, 11, 12
Couples, 1, 3, 19
Creative works, 3
    arts, 70, 79
    literature, 3, 4, 38, 98
    music, 36, 38, 80, 98
    poetry, 21, 36, 98
Creativity, 3, 4, 13, 21, 38, 80, 111, 116
Crisis,
    mid-life, 44
Culture(s), 1, 2, 3, 4, 33, 34, 39, 41, 43, 44, 45, 49, 50, 53, 57, 60, 61, 71, 75, 77, 85, 86, 87, 89, 90, 94, 103, 105, 107, 111
Curse of insight, 7, 83, 97, 98, 99

Subject Index   131

Dean, James, 57, 72, 105
Death, 12, 15, 25, 31, 47, 49, 50, 65, 66, 71, 72, 76, 101, 104
Defenses, 52, 57, 99
Demoralization, 4, 51, 93, 98, 107, 108, 110
Demoralized, 34, 51, 93
Dennett, Daniel,
  Conciousness Explained, 75
Depression, 14, 63, 71, 73, 86, 115
Development, 21
  individual, 74
  life span, 8, 11, 12, 110
Diagnoses, 53
Diagnosis, 21, 22, 31, 34, 39, 95, 99
Dialogue, 23, 24, 27, 101, 102
Differences,
  cultural, 74
  gender, 3, 12, 57, 69, 74
Dilemmas, 2, 94
  universal, 1, 2, 3, 4, 12, 22, 29, 34, 57, 67, 70, 94, 107
Dimensions, 3
  culture, 3, 4, 57, 86
  family, 1, 2, 3, 22, 73, 74, 97
  gender, 57, 74
  hope engendering, 108
  life, 1, 3, 13, 48, 70, 71, 86, 102
  medical, 39, 43, 44, 46, 53
  physical, 39, 43, 71
  psychological, 39, 43, 46, 51, 71
  spiritual, 39, 43, 44, 46, 48, 53, 71, 100
Dinesen, Isak, 5, 28, 48
Divorce(s), 23, 28, 72, 100, 101, 103
Drama(s), 2, 3, 34, 35, 45, 48, 63, 65, 77, 99, 127
Dreams, 2, 7, 8, 25, 36, 38, 53, 54, 83, 94, 99
DSM, (Diagnostic & Statistical manual), 124
  personality disorders, 99
Durst, Will, 78

Ego-active, 80
Ego-receptive, 80

Elders, *See also* Seniors, 4, 91, 94
Emotional fervor, 37
Emotional learning, 2, 34
Emotionality, 1
Empathy, 1, 85, 99
Enduring, 4, 5, 14, 23, 43, 50, 88, 90, 93, 94, 107, 115
Enjoyment, 2
Enmeshed, 22, 23
Entertainment, 4, 7, 36, 48, 64, 71, 80, 83, 94, 113, 126, 127
Environment, 3, 73, 94, 98
Era, 16, 21, 39, 57, 61, 77, 85, 87, 88, 89, 90, 91, 115
Erikson, Erik, 11, 20, 72, 74
  Fidelity, 11
  Identity vs. Identity, 11
  Love, 2, 9, 11, 18, 47, 51, 55, 64, 66, 76, 87, 88, 106, 117, 118, 121
  Wisdom, 11, 50
Event, 99
Evil(s), 48, 49, 50, 69, 70, 71, 78, 115
Experience(s), 1, 3, 5, 13, 15, 31, 33, 34, 37, 44, 45, 46, 48, 60, 67, 68, 74, 77, 82, 89, 90, 99, 106, 107, 110
  life, 1, 3, 13, 48, 70, 71, 86, 102
  vicarious, 3

Family, 1, 2, 3, 6, 16, 17, 21, 22, 23, 24, 25, 26, 27, 28, 29, 31, 32, 41, 49, 52, 53, 57, 59, 62, 63, 71, 73, 74, 84, 89, 93, 96, 97, 98, 101, 103, 104, 105, 109, 110, 123, 127
Family of origin, 3, 22
Fear(s), 6, 13, 34, 36, 37, 38, 39, 53, 59, 62, 70, 83, 85, 88, 94, 98, 110, 119
Films, 9, 13, 22, 30, 32, 37, 44, 49, 50, 53, 60, 64, 68, 69, 72, 85, 91, 102, 104, 112, 124, 125, 126, 127
Fitzgerald, F. Scott, 5
  The Great Gatsby and the American Dream, 5
Folk stories, 4
Folk tales, 94

Forces,
  evil, 71, 115
  good, 5, 7, 11, 13, 15, 18, 19,
    21, 29, 33, 34, 35, 36, 39, 44,
    45, 48, 50, 51, 52, 53, 58, 62,
    65, 66, 70, 71, 72, 73, 75, 76,
    78, 85, 89, 90, 94, 97, 98,
    100, 101, 102, 106, 107, 108,
    110, 113, 115, 125
Frank, Jerome, 8, 51, 54, 97, 107, 108
Freud, Sigmund, 30, 79
Fromm, Erika, 37, 41, 80, 83, 110, 111

Gable, Clark, 73
Generation(s), 19, 22, 23, 25, 33, 57, 58, 59, 62, 66, 71, 85, 87, 88, 89, 90, 91, 107, 116
Generativity, 11, 59, 72, 87
Genuineness, 99
Ghandi, 49, 87, 120
Goals, 11, 70, 109
Grace, 44, 46, 47, 49
Grizzard, Lewis, 78
Growth, 3, 4, 5, 6, 7, 12, 13, 33, 35, 37, 38, 39, 43, 44, 50, 58, 76, 85, 89, 97, 98, 105, 107, 108
Guilt(s), 11, 16, 25, 101, 102
Guilt-ridden, 102

Hammarskjold, Dag, 12
Happiness, 28, 47, 81
Healers, 46, 53
Healing, 43, 44, 46, 97
  setting, 22, 51, 53, 58, 82, 83, 97, 100
Health care, 39, 44, 81, 82
Health, 3, 36, 43, 59, 80
  physical, 39, 43, 65, 71, 80, 81
Hellman, Lillian, 28
  Pentimento, 28
Hermeneutics, 98
History, 3, 20, 24, 36, 50, 77, 79, 82, 85, 89, 110, 111, 123, 125
Holmes, Oliver Wendell, 30
Holocaust, 49
Homo sapiens, 75

Hope engendering, 98, 108
Hopes, 7, 8, 36, 38, 53, 59, 85, 94, 110
  and fears, 2, 3, 7, 8, 85, 94, 97, 99, 107, 116
Humor, 2, 3, 13, 16, 20, 22, 26, 35, 43, 50, 52, 57, 61, 65, 66, 68, 75, 76, 77, 80, 82, 83, 85, 87, 88, 103, 106, 116
Hungers, 75, 83
Hypochondriacs, 45

Identity, 15, 21, 59, 72
  cultural, 62
  family, 3, 22, 73, 74, 97
  person, 2, 3, 5, 6, 7, 11, 12, 13, 21, 22, 23, 30, 35, 41, 47, 51, 52, 58, 73, 85, 93, 96, 97
Illness, 9, 30, 32, 44, 45, 47, 59, 90, 91, 112, 124
Imago, 94
Impact on others, 99
Impediments, 4, 107
Impulses,
  libidinal, 70
In Order of Importance, 30
Individuate, 22
Individuation, 22
Industry, 11, 86, 89
Infidelity, 9, 103, 111
Influences,
  cultural, 62
  relational, 2, 22, 52, 95, 100, 101
Information, 37, 95, 97, 109, 110, 125, 127
Initiative, 11, 16
Insight, 3, 5, 7, 11, 69, 75, 80, 83, 85, 98, 99, 105, 110
Inspiration, 50, 85
Integrity, 11, 59, 60, 100, 101, 113
Interpersonal, 51
  style, see also Patterns, 5, 7, 38, 48, 52, 72, 73, 86, 95, 99, 105, 106
Intimacy, 3, 6, 7, 9, 11, 14, 17, 21, 22, 23, 25, 67, 72, 74, 108, 111

Subject Index 133

Issues, 21, 74, 91
   racial, 60, 61, 62
James, William, 2, 90
Journeys, 106

Keats, John, 36
   A Thing of Beauty, 36
Killer(s), 62, 124, 126
Kopp, Sheldon, 106, 107, 111

Label(s), 57, 80, 90, 99
Lazarus, Arnold, 100
   Basic Id, 100, 110
L-Dopa (Levodopa), 45
Learned optimism, 84, 107, 108, 111
Learning, 2, 12, 15, 35, 40, 67, 81, 94, 95, 97, 98, 110, 111
Lee, Spike, 61, 62, 77
Leitmotifs, 11
Lewis, Richard, 78
Life bets, 11, 12, 98
Life, 1, 3, 13, 48, 70, 71, 86, 94, 102
   challenges, 11, 12, 86, 93
   hunches, 12, 44
   stages, See also Erikson, 1, 3, 5, 9, 12, 16, 20, 34, 37, 39, 43, 54, 57, 70, 71, 72, 73, 89, 93, 95, 110
   stories, 2, 30, 97, 106
   universal, 1, 2, 3, 4, 12, 22, 29, 34, 57, 67, 70, 94, 107
Livingston, Gordon, 89, 91
Lizard brain, 37
Locus of control, 106
Loss(es), 3, 32, 39, 41, 55, 71, 85, 89, 91, 96, 98, 110, 112
Love, 2, 5, 6, 8, 9, 11, 14, 15, 17, 18, 19, 21, 22, 41, 44, 47, 50, 51, 54, 55, 61, 63, 64, 66, 67, 69, 71, 72, 74, 76, 77, 78, 79, 80, 86, 87, 88, 104, 106, 117, 118, 121

Managed care, 39, 54, 82, 96, 98, 99, 110
Marriage, 23, 73
   dysfunctional, 27, 76, 104

Maturity, 6, 30, 72, 113
Maugham, W. Somerset, 34
Memories, 19, 22, 38, 53, 54, 83, 85, 89, 91
Men, 3, 8, 9, 14, 19, 20, 25, 26, 40, 41, 61, 64, 68, 69, 71, 72, 73, 74, 78, 86, 88, 104, 105, 106, 113, 119
Mental health, 97
Messages, 37, 38, 49, 71, 88
Metaphor(s), 8, 13, 18, 36, 41, 48, 52, 53, 98, 106, 107, 116
   Therapy, 41, 46, 52, 74, 98, 102, 104, 105, 106, 123
Mind, 30, 43, 70
   and body, 80, 81
Minimal interference principle, 4, 35, 39, 93, 96, 100
Mistakes, 102, 104, 125
Motivations, 2, 7, 11, 13, 44, 53, 74, 83, 94, 97, 98
Motives, 7, 12, 38, 48, 57, 65, 76
Mottoes, 97
Movie(s), 1, 2, 3, 4, 5, 7, 8, 9, 12, 13, 14, 15, 17, 20, 21, 22, 24, 25, 26, 27, 29, 30, 31, 32, 33, 34, 35, 36, 37, 38, 39, 40, 43, 44, 45, 46, 48, 49, 50, 52, 53, 57, 58, 59, 60, 61, 62, 63, 64, 65, 66, 67, 68, 69, 70, 71, 72, 73, 74, 75, 76, 77, 78, 79, 80, 82, 83, 85, 86, 87, 88, 89, 90, 91, 93, 94, 95, 96, 97, 98, 99, 100, 101, 102, 103, 104, 105, 106, 107, 112, 113, 115, 116, 123, 124, 125, 126, 127
Mowrer, Hobart, 1, 111
Murderer, 47, 48
Music, 6, 21, 24, 36, 37, 38, 45, 47, 61, 62, 63, 80, 86, 89, 90, 98, 104, 117, 118, 120, 126
Myths, 4, 8, 9, 65, 75, 87

Napier, Gus, 6, 30, 73
   The Family Crucible, 30
Narcissism, 26, 71
Neurolinguistic programming, 37
Neurolinguistic programming, sensory, 37, 38, 80
Neurotic, 1, 55, 72, 86, 94, 102

Subject Index

Neurotic paradox, 1, 94
Newman, Paul, 17, 40, 58, 71, 72, 105
Niehbur, Rheinhold,
   We Must Be Saved, 50

Pain, 77, 81
Paine, Thomas, 30
Paradox,
   see also *Neurotic*, 55, 86
Pathology, 12, 104
Pathos, 2, 16
Patient(s), 3, 4, 7, 13, 16, 21, 39, 45, 51, 52, 53, 54, 58, 72, 76, 81, 82, 90, 93, 95, 96, 97, 98, 99, 100, 101, 104, 106, 109, 110, 111, 118, 121, 124
Patterns,
   of change, 98
   see also interpersonal style, 7, 54, 95
Pentimento, 28
Personality, 32, 67, 79, 99
Perspective(s), 1, 2, 4, 6, 8, 11, 12, 13, 20, 21, 30, 31, 34, 35, 44, 46, 49, 51, 53, 54, 59, 63, 65, 66, 67, 72, 77, 78, 81, 83, 87, 89, 94, 96, 97, 98, 99, 106, 107, 111, 123
Phases, 3, 5, 40, 90, 95
Pittman, Frank, 9, 71, 74, 105, 111
Plot(s), 4, 17, 57, 61, 96, 97, 115, 125, 127
Poems,
   on the Underground, 36, 37
Poetry, 21, 36, 98
Popcorn, 38, 72, 78, 113
Pornography,
   prurient, 76, 77
Power(s), 7, 8, 33, 41, 47, 48, 49, 70, 100
   healing, 3, 4, 8, 13, 20, 37, 39, 43, 44, 45, 46, 48, 51, 53, 54, 73, 76, 82, 97, 98, 99, 101, 107, 108, 110
Practitioners, 81, 97
Prevention, 39, 80, 81, 82
Principle(s), 1, 2, 3, 4, 13, 21, 37, 53, 80, 93, 94, 96

creativity, 3, 111, 116
   See also Minimal interference, 4
Problems, 35, 38, 96, 98
   stress-related, 81, 82
Process(es), 2, 3, 4, 5, 6, 7, 11, 12, 13, 17, 21, 35, 38, 41, 43, 80, 81, 83, 90, 93, 94, 95, 96, 97, 99, 101, 107, 110, 111
   creative, 19, 34
   healing, 43, 44, 97
   left-brain, 37, 80
   of change, 98, 107
   right-brain, 37, 80
Professionals, 1, 33, 39, 43, 82, 85, 95
Promiscuity, 78
Prurient interest, 77
Psyche, 43, 44, 81, 123
Psychiatrist, 3, 22, 24, 26, 35, 43, 46, 71, 89, 94, 103, 104, 105
Psychologist, 1, 2, 9, 12, 41, 53, 102, 107, 111
Psychology, 2, 3, 5, 8, 12, 20, 32, 34, 36, 37, 39, 41, 44, 47, 50, 54, 55, 83, 84, 91, 94, 102, 110, 111
Psychopathology, 9, 30, 32, 91, 104, 112, 124
Psychophysiological, 80, 81
Psychophysiological disorders, 81
Psychophysiological,
   reconditioning, 80
Psychosis, 102
Psychosomatic, 81, 82, 83
Psychotherapy, 8, 41, 51, 79, 95
   *see also*Therapy, 41, 46, 52, 74, 98, 102, 104, 105, 106, 123
Puer eternis, 90
Puzzles, 1, 2, 34, 35, 53, 57, 65, 107

Qualities, 97
   crucial (for effective therapy), 6, 38, 51, 61, 95, 96, 97, 98, 108
   of change, 4, 5, 21, 98, 107

Rape, 49
References, 46, 67, 105, 123
Rehabilitation, 39

Relations, relationships, 2, 3, 5, 7, 20, 23, 54, 64, 69, 95
   healing, 43, 44, 97
   therapeutic, 9, 12, 32, 52, 99
Relaxation, 81, 83
Religion, 3, 18, 39, 44, 54, 55
Religious themes,
   The Shaking of the Foundations, 49
Renoir, Jean, 73
Research, 33, 51, 64, 68, 81, 82, 83, 84, 85, 111
Researchers, 81, 82
Resources, 2, 4, 13, 31, 33, 34, 39, 64, 90, 94, 107, 109, 111, 123
Responsibility, 15, 71, 96, 99
Reversal, 6, 94
Rewrite, rewriting, 36, 40, 79, 93, 96, 98, 100
   life stories, 2, 40, 96, 100, 107
Rhetoric, 98
Ritual, 51, 97
Rogers, Will, 46
Role(s), 5, 8, 22, 25, 26, 34, 35, 43, 52, 54, 60, 62, 70, 71, 72, 74, 75, 86, 89, 94, 95, 97, 103, 104, 105
   transference, 52, 95
Rudner, Rita, 68, 69, 74
Rules, 15, 25, 34, 52, 54, 67, 73

Scaffolding & rebuilding, 13
Schemes, 60, 99
Schizophrenia, 53, 87
Science, 3, 9, 30, 32, 41, 45, 47, 54, 82, 83, 84, 110, 111, 127
Secret(s), 7, 19, 20, 29, 37, 38, 64, 70, 84
Self-actualization, 76
Self-defeating,
   patterns, 1, 2, 4, 5, 7, 26, 52, 74, 83, 98, 99
Self-determination, 106
Self-disclosure, 59, 101
Self-esteem, 71
Senses, 37, 38, 72, 116
Sensory channels,
   auditory, 80
   tactile, 37, 80
   visual, 33, 37, 38, 49, 80
Serenity Prayer, 50
Serial killer, 62, 66, 124
Sex, 5, 6, 8, 22, 26, 35, 47, 54, 57, 61, 65, 66, 67, 74, 76, 77, 78, 88
Sexuality, 67, 69, 77, 78
Shadows, 22, 105
Shandling, Gary, 78
Shaw, George Bernard, 105
Shrinks, 81, 94, 102
Sinclair, Upton, 83
Skills,
   professional, 1, 31, 102, 105, 110
Society, 15, 16, 38, 43, 44, 46, 57, 71, 77, 120, 123
Solutions, 1, 2, 13, 34, 35, 38, 53, 61, 94, 98, 99, 105
Soma, 43, 81
Soul, 2, 7, 8, 30, 43, 45, 54, 57, 60, 72
Spectrum, 12, 80
Spirit of the times, 36, 44, 89
Stability, 73
Stage(s), 1, 2, 3, 5, 6, 7, 8, 9, 11, 12, 13, 14, 16, 18, 20, 31, 34, 37, 39, 43, 54, 57, 70, 71, 72, 73, 88, 89, 90, 93, 95, 96, 99, 110
   of consciousness, 65
   of relationships, 12, 54
   predictable, 3, 5, 34, 35, 57, 67, 95, 99
State(s), 31, 39, 41, 51, 80, 81, 83, 90, 107, 110, 111
Steinem, Gloria, 13
Story(ies), 2, 4, 8, 9, 14, 15, 16, 19, 20, 21, 22, 23, 28, 29, 30, 31, 33, 34, 35, 36, 39, 41, 43, 45, 46, 48, 49, 52, 53, 54, 55, 60, 61, 65, 67, 69, 70, 71, 76, 78, 79, 86, 90, 93, 94, 96, 97, 98, 100, 101, 102, 104, 105, 106, 107, 115, 116, 117, 118, 120, 125
   life, 1, 2, 3, 4, 5, 8, 9, 11, 12, 13, 14, 17, 18, 19, 20, 21, 22, 26, 31, 34, 35, 37, 39, 41, 43, 44, 45, 47, 48, 49, 51, 54, 57, 58,

59, 61, 62, 64, 65, 67, 68, 70, 71, 73, 74, 80, 81, 83, 86, 89, 90, 91, 93, 94, 96, 98, 99, 100, 102, 104, 107, 110, 113, 115
Storytelling, 43
Strategy(ies), 1, 7, 8, 12, 13, 31, 35, 37, 38, 51, 52, 54, 57, 64, 70, 74, 77, 93, 94, 95, 96, 97, 98, 99, 101, 105, 109

valence, 6, 52, 54, 95

Movie Index

5 Easy Pieces, 25
A Beautiful Mind, 102, 121
A Few Good Men, 26
A Man for All Seasons, 52, 100, 120
A River Runs Through It, 17, 25
A Thousand Clowns, 16, 58
A Walk in the Clouds, 20, 21, 40
After Hours, 14
Age Old Friends, 20, 25
American Beauty, 48, 121
Amistad, 46
Analyze This, 101
Article 99, 45
Awakenings, 45

Basic Instinct, 102
Being There, 35, 76
Beyond Therapy, 102
Birth of a Nation, 86, 117
Black Stallion, 14
Blackboard Jungle, 63
Body Heat, 26, 118
Boys in the Band, 69
Brigadoon (a musical), 106

California Split, 89
Carnal Knowledge, 25
Cider House Rules, 52, 67
City Slickers, 19
Columbo, 52
Crimes of the Heart, 65
Crooklyn, 62
Curly Sue, 17

Dead Man Walking, 47
Deconstructing Harry, 103
Do the Right Thing, 61
Don Juan DeMarco, 103
Driving Miss Daisy, 40, 67, 120

Easy Rider, 17, 25, 118
Elephant Man, 46, 120

Fried Green Tomatoes, 19, 40
Girl 6, 61, 77
Girl Interrupted, 53, 90
Good Will Hunting, 101
Gosford Park, 89, 113
Guess Who's Coming to Dinner, 60, 118, 119

Harvey, 72

Instinct, 103
Judgment at Nuremberg, 89
Jungle Fever, 61

Kansas City, 89

Lantana, 113
Little Voice, 59
Look Who's Talking, 14
Look Who's Talking, Too, 15
Lysistrata (a Roman play), 77

M*A*S*H, 45, 88, 118
Malcolm X, 62
Michael, 48
Mining for Stories, 36
Mr. Smith Goes to Washington, 25, 117
My Beautiful Launderette, 69

National Lampoon's Animal House, 88
Nobody's Fool, 19, 58, 72
Norma Rae, 66
Now and Then, 65

Of Mice and Men, 14
Oh Brother Where Art Thou?, 62
One Flew Over the Cuckoo's Nest, 16, 25, 104, 120
Ordinary People, 16, 73, 101, 120

Patch Adams, 45
Phenomenon, 48
Philadelphia, 66, 69
Psycho, 103, 104, 116, 117

Rebel Without a Cause, 57, 72, 118

School Daze, 62
Sea of Love, 66
Shadowlands, 47, 121
Shirley Valentine, 18, 65
Shrek, 113

Smoke Signals, 63
Something to Talk About, 66
Stand By Me, 15
Star Wars, 69, 70, 71, 114, 117
Summer of Sam, 62
Tender Mercies, 19, 47, 59

Terms of Endearment, 20, 26, 47, 66, 120
The Apprenticeship of Dudy Kravitz, 60
The Cabinet of Dr. Daligari, 104
The Citadel, 45
The Dance Away Lover, 5, 7
The Doctor, 45
The First Wives Club, 66
The Green Mile, 48
The Hospital, 19, 44
The Last of His Tribe, 20, 40, 71, 77, 89
The Marx Brothers (movies), 87, 88
The Milagro Beanfield War, 63
The Prince of Tides, 104
The Red Neck Way of Knowledge, 36
The Shining, 25
The Story of Us, 23, 101
The Trip to Bountiful, 40, 59
The Verdict, 16, 17, 19, 72
The War of the Roses, 104
The Witches of Eastwick, 67
The Young Poisoner's Handbook, 104
Thelma and Louise, 65, 66
Through a Glass Darkly, 53
Tin Cup, 102
To Kill a Mockingbird, 16, 25, 49, 60, 115, 117
Torch Song Trilogy, 69
Toy Story, 29
Twelve Angry Men, 104

Under the Sand, 113

What About Bob?, 52
What Women Want, 25

When Harry Met Sally, 73, 113, 117
Wild Strawberries, 20, 25, 124
Wizard of Oz, 106, 107, 117

About the Author

THOMAS H. PEAKE is Professor of Psychology at Florida Tech and an adjunct professor at the Florida Mental Health Institute. Licensed in three states and England, he has trained health professionals and practiced clinical psychology for over twenty years. His publication and practice areas include books and articles in psychotherapy, clinical training, medical psychology, couples therapy, and healthy aging. He is the author of *Healthy Aging, Healthy Treatment: The Impact of Telling Stories* (Praeger, 1998).

616.8914 P357c

Peake, Tom H.

Cinema and life development